BASICS OF KEYBOARD THEORY

LEVEL VI

Fourth Edition

Julie McIntosh Johnson

J. Johnson Music Publications

5062 Siesta Lane
Yorba Linda, CA 92886
Phone: (714) 961-0257
Fax: (714) 242-9350
www.bktmusic.com
info@bktmusic.com

Fourth Edition ©1997, Julie McIntosh Johnson
Previous Editions © 1983, 1992, Julie McIntosh Johnson

Basics of Keyboard Theory, Level VI, Fourth Edition

Published by:

J. Johnson Music Publications
5062 Siesta Ln.
Yorba Linda, CA 92886 U.S.A.
(714) 961-0257

All rights reserved. No part of this book may be reproduced or transmitted in any form or by any means, electronic or mechanical, including photocopying, recording, or by any information storage and retrieval system without written permission from the author, except for the inclusion of brief quotations in a review.

©1997 by Julie McIntosh Johnson. Revised.
Previous editions ©1983, 1992, Julie McIntosh Johnson.
Printed in United States of America

Library of Congress Cataloging in Publication Data

Johnson, Julie Anne McIntosh
Basics of Keyboard Theory, Level VI, Fourth Edition

ISBN 1-891757-06-7 Softcover

LC TX 4-721-498

TO THE TEACHER

Intended as a supplement to private or group music lessons, *Basics of Keyboard Theory, Level VI* presents basic theory concepts to the advanced intermediate music student. This level is to be used with the student who has had approximately six to seven years of music lessons, and is playing piano literature at the level of Kuhlau's *Sonatina, Op. 55, No. 1*, or Grieg's *Puck*.

Basics of Keyboard Theory, Level VI is divided into seventeen lessons, with two reviews, and a test at the end. Application of each theory concept is made to piano music of the student's level. Lessons may be combined with one another or divided into smaller sections, depending on the ability of the student. Whenever possible, it is helpful to demonstrate theory concepts on the keyboard, and apply them to the music the student is playing.

Learning music theory can be a very rewarding experience for the student when carefully applied to lessons. *Basics of Keyboard Theory, Level VI*, is an important part of learning this valuable subject.

BASICS OF KEYBOARD THEORY
COMPUTER ACTIVITIES
by
Nancy Plourde
with
Julie McIntosh Johnson and Anita Yee Belansky

Colorful, exciting games that reinforce Basics of Keyboard Theory lessons!

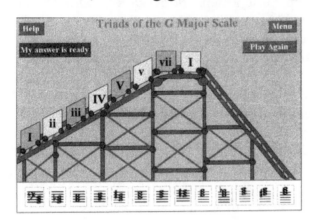

LEVELS PREPARATORY, 1, and 2: 30 GAMES, 10 PER LEVEL!
LEVELS 3 and 4: 20 GAMES, 10 PER LEVEL!
LEVELS 5 and 6: 20 GAMES, 10 PER LEVEL!
Corresponds with MTAC CM Syllabus & *Basics of Keyboard Theory* books, or may be used independently.

Download a free demo at www.pbjmusic.com
---**Order Form**---

Name_____

Address_____

City_____State_____Zip_____

Email_____Phone_____

Mail to: PBJ Music Publications
5062 Siesta Ln.
Yorba Linda, CA 92886
(714) 961-0257

Qty		Cost
_____	Levels Prep-II, Mac/PC: $49.95	_____
_____	Levels III-IV, Mac/PC: $39.95	_____
_____	Levels 5-6, PC only: $49.95	_____
	Sub Total:	_____
	Sales Tax (CA, AZ, TX residents)	_____
	Shipping:	$5.00
	Total:	_____

System Requirements
<u>IBM or compatible:</u> 486 33 MHz or higher, Windows 3.1, 95, 98, NT, or XP, 8 MB RAM, 5 MB hard disk space, MIDI Soundcard, VGA monitor.
<u>Macintosh:</u> System 7 or greater, 8 MB RAM, 3 MB hard disk space available, color monitor.

TABLE OF CONTENTS

Lesson 1: Major and Minor Key Signatures...1

Lesson 2: Major and Minor Scales...11

Lesson 3: Intervals..17

Lesson 4: Major, Minor, Augmented, and Diminished Triads and Inversions.....................21

Lesson 5: Primary and Secondary Triads..29

Lesson 6: The Dominant Seventh Chord...37

Lesson 7: Authentic, Half, Plagal, and Deceptive Cadences..41

Review: Words Used in Lessons 1-7...49

Review: Lessons 1-7..51

Lesson 8: Time Signatures...59

Lesson 9: Signs and Terms..67

Lesson 10: Motive; Repetition, Imitation, Sequence...75

Lesson 11: Transposition...79

Lesson 12: Modulation..81

Lesson 13: The Four Periods of Music History; The Baroque Period...................................83

Lesson 14: The Classical Period...87

Lesson 15: The Romantic Period..93

Lesson 16: The Contemporary Period...97

Review: Lessons 8-16..101

Review Test...105

Basics of Keyboard Theory is dedicated to my husband Rob, without whose love, support, help, and incredible patience, this series would not have been possible.

LESSON 1
MAJOR AND MINOR KEY SIGNATURES

The **KEY SIGNATURE** for a musical composition is found at the beginning of the piece, next to the clef signs.

The **KEY SIGNATURE** tells you two things:

1. The **key** or **tonality** of the music.

2. **Which notes** in the music are to **receive sharps or flats**.

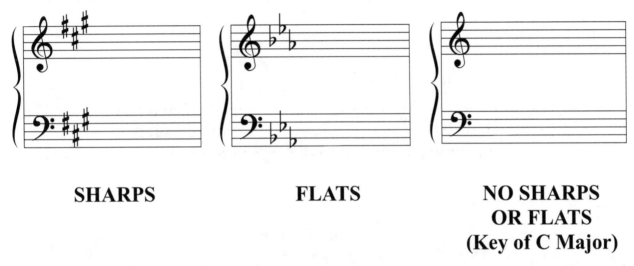

SHARPS　　　　　　**FLATS**　　　　　　**NO SHARPS
OR FLATS
(Key of C Major)**

If the key signature has **SHARPS**, they will be written in this order, on these lines and spaces. This is called the **ORDER OF SHARPS.**

FCGDAEB

A saying to help you remember this order is:

Fat Cats Go Down Alleys Eating Bologna

If a key signature has one sharp, it will be F♯. If a key signature has two sharps, they will be F♯ and C♯, etc.

To determine which Major key a group of sharps represents, find and name the last sharp (the sharp furthest to the right), then go up a half step from that sharp. The note which is a half step above the last sharp is the name of the Major key.

Three sharps: F♯, C♯, G♯

Last sharp is G♯

A half step above G♯ is A

Key of A Major

To determine which sharps are in a Major key, find the sharp which is a half step below the name of the key. Name all the sharps from the Order of Sharps up to and including that sharp.

Key of D Major

A half step below D is C♯

Name all sharps, from the Order of Sharps, up to and including C♯

F♯ and C♯

If a key signature has flats, they will be in the following order, written on these lines and spaces. This is called the **ORDER OF FLATS.**

BEADGCF

THE ORDER OF FLATS

The Order of Flats can be memorized this way:

BEAD Gum Candy Fruit

If a key signature has one flat, it will be B♭. If it has two flats, they will be B♭ and E♭, etc.

To determine which Major key a group of flats represents, simply name the next to last flat.

Three flats: B♭, E♭, A♭

Next to last flat is E♭

Key of E♭ Major

To determine which flats are needed for a given key, name all the flats from the Order of Flats up to and including the name of the key, then add one more.

Key of E♭ Major

Name all flats from the Order of Flats up to and including E♭, then add one more.

B♭, E♭, A♭

The key signature for F Major has to be memorized. It has one flat: B♭.

KEY SIGNATURE FOR F MAJOR

Major keys which have sharps will be named with a letter only, or a letter and a sharp (for example, G Major, D Major, F♯ Major).

Major keys which have flats will have a flat in their name (for example, B♭ Major, D♭ Major, E♭ Major).

The two exceptions to the above rules are F Major (one flat: B♭), and C Major (no sharps or flats).

1. Name these Major keys.

_____   _____   _____   _____   _____

_____   _____   _____   _____   _____

_____   _____   _____   _____   _____

2. Write the key signatures for these Major keys.

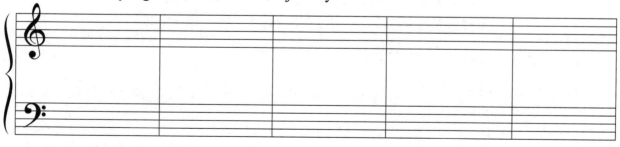

G Major   F♯ Major   F Major   D Major   B Major

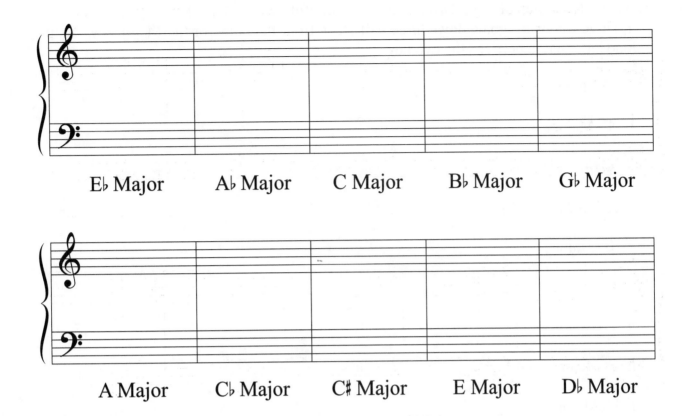

Eb Major   Ab Major   C Major   Bb Major   Gb Major

A Major   Cb Major   C# Major   E Major   Db Major

Most Major key signatures have **RELATIVE MINORS.** The relative minor is found by going down three half steps from the name of the Major key. Skip one letter between the names of the keys.

KEY SIGNATURE FOR D MAJOR
THREE HALF STEPS BELOW D IS B
KEY OF B MINOR

One way to determine whether a composition is in the Major or minor key is to look at the last note of the piece. It is usually the same as the name of the key. (For example, a piece which is in the key of e minor will probably end on E.) Also, look at the music to find the note around which the music appears to be centered; which note appears to be the main note of the piece. This should be the same as the name of the key.

3. Write the names of the relative minors for the following Major keys. (Determine the relative minor by going <u>down</u> three half steps from the name of the Major key. Skip one letter name between the two keys.)

a. G Major _____

b. E♭ Major _____

c. C Major _____

d. F Major _____

e. B♭ Major _____

f. D Major _____

g. A♭ Major _____

h. A Major _____

i. D♭ Major _____

4. Give the name of the relative Major for each of the following minor keys. (Determine the relative Major by going <u>up</u> three half steps. Skip one letter name between the names of the keys.)

a. d minor _____

b. e minor _____

c. f minor _____

d. c minor _____

e. a minor _____

f. f♯ minor _____

g. g minor _____

h. b minor _____

i. b♭ minor _____

5. Name these minor keys. (Determine the Major key name, then go down three half steps to find the relative minor.)

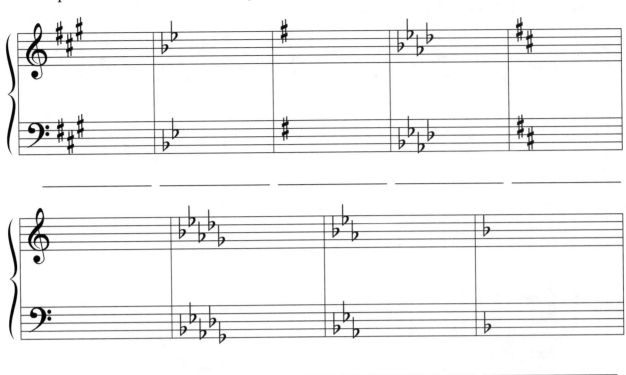

_____ _____ _____ _____ _____

_____ _____ _____ _____

6. Write the key signatures for these minor keys. (Go <u>up</u> three half steps to find the relative Major, then write the key signature for that Major key.)

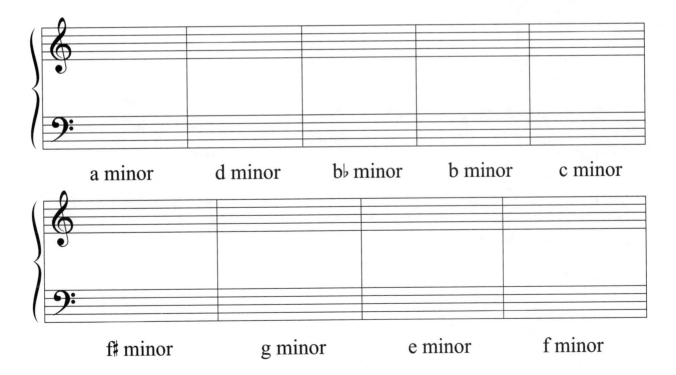

a minor   d minor   b♭ minor   b minor   c minor

f♯ minor   g minor   e minor   f minor

7. Name the Major or minor key signature for each of the following musical examples.

a. From *Short Prelude #3* by J.S. Bach. _____

b. From *Für Elise* by Beethoven. _____

c. From *Polka* by Tchaikovsky. _____

d. From *Sonata, L. 58*, by Scarlatti. _____

e. From *Dance, Op. 60, No. 2*, by Kabalevsky. _____

f. From *Ecossaise, K. Wo083*, by Beethoven. _____

8. Memorize these key signature.

C Major and a minor: no sharps or flats

G Major and e minor: F♯

D Major and b minor: F♯ and C♯

A Major and f♯ minor: F♯, C♯, and G♯

E Major: F♯, C♯, G♯, and D♯

B Major: F♯, C♯, G♯, D♯, and A♯

F♯ Major: F♯, C♯, G♯, D♯, A♯, and E♯

C♯ Major: F♯, C♯, G♯, D♯, A♯, E♯, and B♯

F Major and d minor: B♭

B♭ Major and g minor: B♭, and E♭

E♭ Major and c minor: B♭, E♭, and A♭

A♭ Major and f minor: B♭, E♭, A♭, and D♭

D♭ Major and b♭ minor: B♭, E♭, A♭, D♭, and G♭

G♭ Major: B♭, E♭, A♭, D♭, G♭, and C♭

C♭ Major: B♭, E♭, A♭, D♭, G♭, C♭, and F♭

LESSON 2
MAJOR AND MINOR SCALES

SCALES are a series of eight notes, which are each a step apart. They begin and end with notes of the same letter name.

MAJOR SCALES contain all the sharps or flats from the Major key signature with the same name.

Example: D Major Scale begins and ends with the note "D," and has F♯ and C♯. (In Major scales, most of the steps are whole steps, with half steps occurring between notes 3-4 and 7-8.)

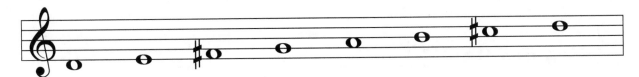

D MAJOR SCALE

There are several forms of minor scales. Two of these are **Natural Minor** and **Harmonic Minor.**

NATURAL MINOR SCALES contain all the sharps or flats from the minor key signature with the same letter name.

Example: d natural minor scale begins and ends with the note "D," and has B♭.

D NATURAL MINOR SCALE

HARMONIC MINOR SCALES are created by raising the 7th note of the natural minor scale a half step. This creates a half step, rather than a whole step, between the 7th and 8th notes of the scale, making the 7th note a "leading tone."

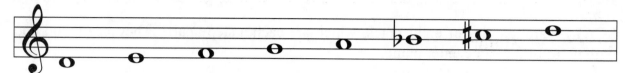

D HARMONIC MINOR SCALE

The **CHROMATIC SCALE** is a series of 13 notes. Each note is a half step away from its neighbor. When writing the Chromatic Scale on the staff, sharps are used when the scale is ascending, and flats are used when the scale is descending.

CHROMATIC SCALE BEGINNING ON F

1. Write these scales.

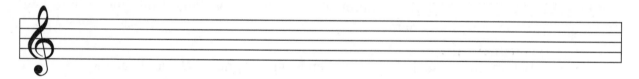

Cb Major

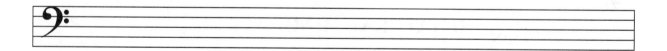

B Major

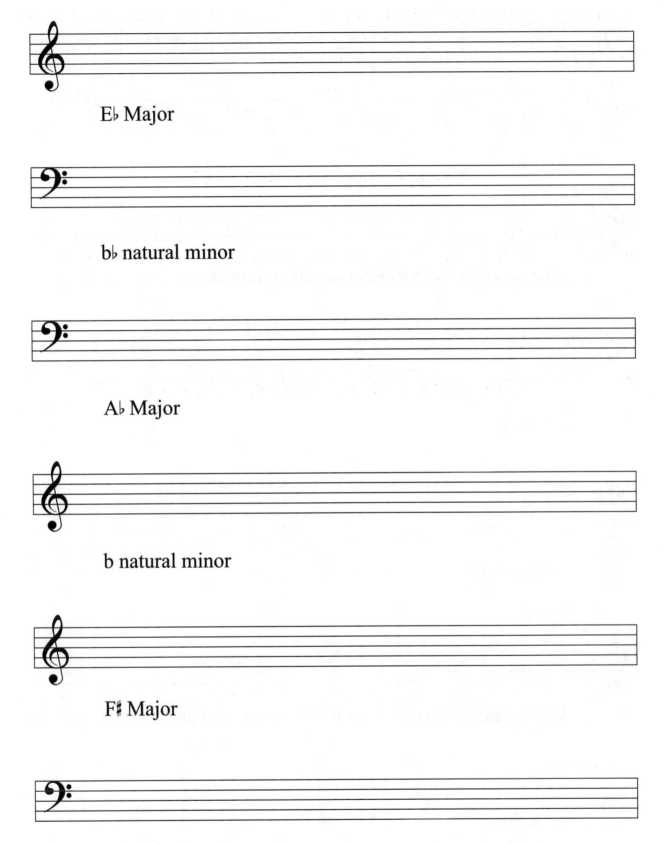

E♭ Major

b♭ natural minor

A♭ Major

b natural minor

F♯ Major

g harmonic minor

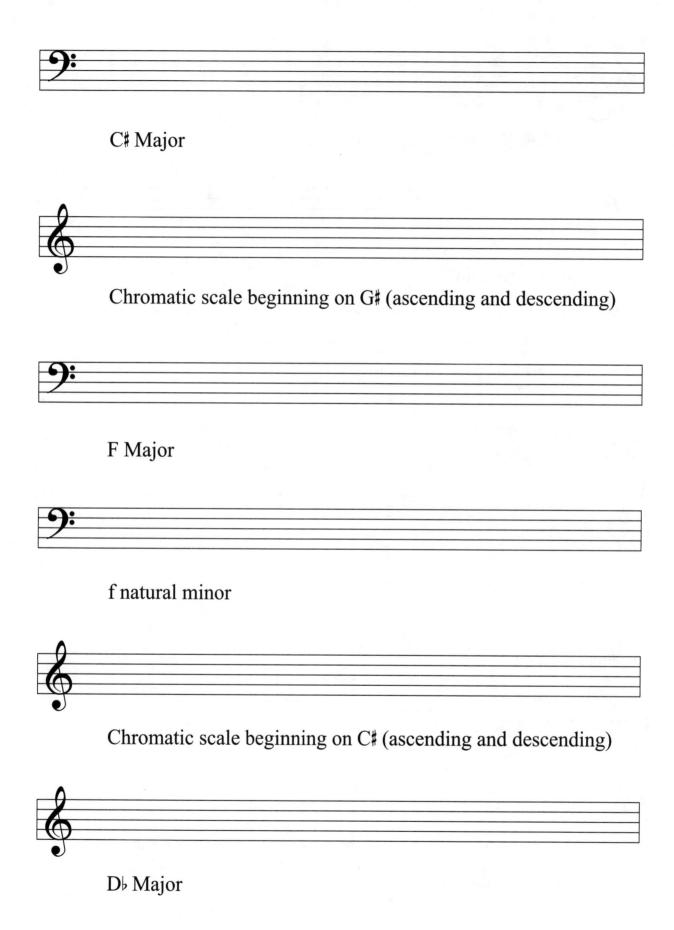

C♯ Major

Chromatic scale beginning on G♯ (ascending and descending)

F Major

f natural minor

Chromatic scale beginning on C♯ (ascending and descending)

D♭ Major

Chromatic scale beginning on E (ascending and descending)

2. Give the name and type of each circled scale in the examples below. For minor scales, be sure to put which form of minor is used.

a. From *Ecossaise, K. Wo083,* No. 6, by Beethoven. _____ _____ Scale

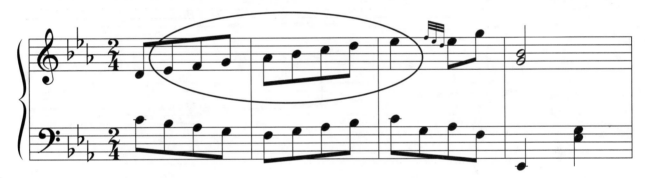

b. From *Sonata, L. 58,* by Scarlatti. _____ _____ Scale

c.. From *Dance, Op. 60, No. 2,* by Kavalevsky. _____ _____ Scale

d. From *Song, Op. 60, No. 3*, by Kavalevsky. _____ _____ Scale

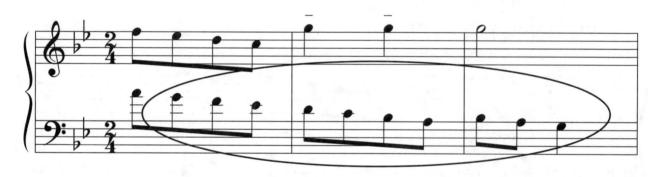

e. From *Sonata, Op. 55, No. 1: Vivace,* by Kuhlau. _____ _____ Scale

LESSON 3
INTERVALS

An **INTERVAL** is the distance between two notes. Intervals are named with numbers.

When naming intervals, count the two notes that make the interval, and all the lines and spaces, or all the letter names, between the two notes.

If the top note of the interval is within the key of the bottom note, the interval is **Major** or **Perfect.** 2nds, 3rds, 6ths, and 7ths are Major, and 4ths, 5ths, and 8ths are Perfect.

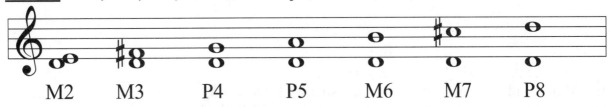

To write a Major or Perfect interval above a given note, determine the key signature for the lower note, and write any accidentals that are in the key signature before the upper note.

To write a Major or Perfect interval below a given note, determine all possibilities the note could be. Choose the key that contains the given upper note.

In the example below, a M7 below C is needed. The three possibilities are D, D♭, and D♯. The key of D♭ Major has C, D Major has C♯, and D♯ has C double sharp. The answer, therefore, is D♭.

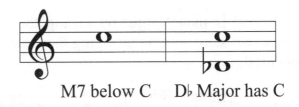

If a Major 2nd, 3rd, 6th, or 7th is made smaller by lowering the top note or raising the bottom note a half step, without changing the letter name of either note, the interval becomes **minor.**

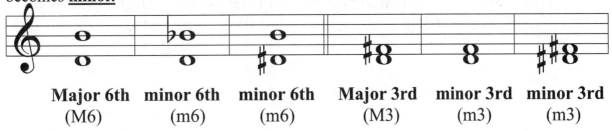

If a Perfect 4th, 5th, or 8th is made smaller by lowering the top note a half step, or raising the bottom note a half step, without changing the letter name of either note, the interval becomes **<u>diminished.</u>**

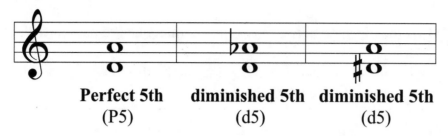

Perfect 5th	**diminished 5th**	**diminished 5th**
(P5)	(d5)	(d5)

If a Major 2nd, 3rd, 6th, or 7th is made smaller by lowering the top note a <u>whole</u> step, or raising the bottom note a whole step, without changing the letter name of either note, the interval becomes **<u>diminished.</u>**

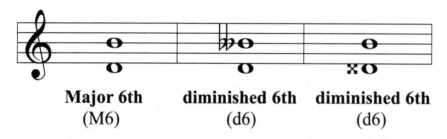

Major 6th	**diminished 6th**	**diminished 6th**
(M6)	(d6)	(d6)

If a Major or Perfect interval is made larger by raising the top note a half step, or lowering the bottom note a half step, without changing the letter name of either note, the interval becomes **<u>Augmented.</u>**

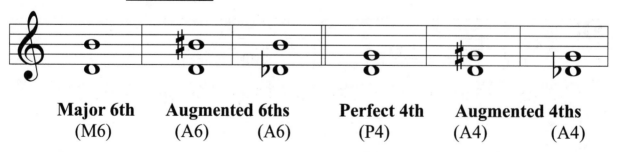

Major 6th	**Augmented 6ths**		**Perfect 4th**	**Augmented 4ths**	
(M6)	(A6)	(A6)	(P4)	(A4)	(A4)

1. Name these intervals. Give their qualities (Major, Perfect, minor, Augmented, or diminished), and number names (2nd, 3rd, etc.) The first one is given.

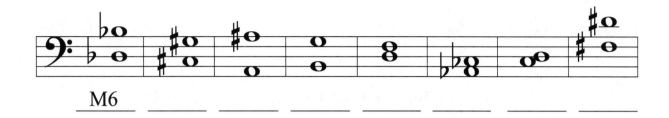

M6 ___ ___ ___ ___ ___ ___ ___ ___

___ ___ ___ ___ ___ ___ ___ ___

2. Complete these intervals. Do not change the given note.

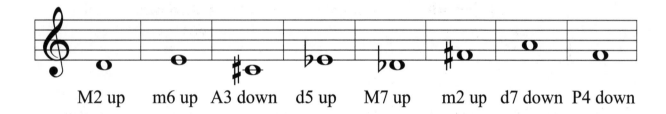

M2 up   m6 up   A3 down   d5 up   M7 up   m2 up   d7 down   P4 down

A3 up   d3 up   A2 down   d4 down   P5 up   M6 up   A4 down   P8 up

When naming intervals within a piece of music, follow these steps:

a. Write the sharps or flats from the key signature in front of the notes. (This way, you will not forget to consider them while naming the interval.)

b. Determine the number for the interval (by counting the lines and spaces, or the letter names.)

c. Using the key signature for the <u>lowest</u> note of the interval, find the quality (Major, minor, Perfect, diminished, or Augmented).

3. Name the circled intervals in the passages below. Follow the steps listed above for each interval.

a. From *Tarantella* by Prokofiev.

b. From *Puck* by Grieg.

c. From *Norse Song* by Schumann.

LESSON 4
MAJOR, MINOR AUGMENTED AND DIMINISHED TRIADS AND INVERSIONS

A **TRIAD** is a three note chord.

D Major Triad

MAJOR TRIADS are made up of the first, third, and fifth notes of the Major scale with the same letter name. The lowest note of a Major triad in root position (with the notes each a third apart) names the triad.

D Major Scale

Block   Broken
D Major Triad

To change a Major triad into a **MINOR** triad, lower the middle note (the third) a half step. Minor triads have the same sharps or flats found in the minor key signature with the same letter name.

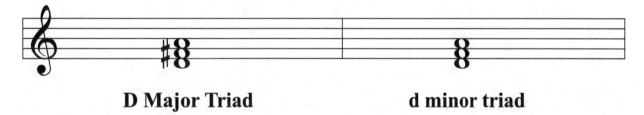

D Major Triad   **d minor triad**

To change a Major triad into an **AUGMENTED** triad, raise the top note (the fifth) a half step. The intervals between the notes are both Major 3rds.

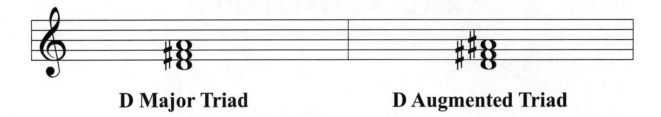

D Major Triad   **D Augmented Triad**

To change a Major triad into a **DIMINISHED** triad, lower the middle note (the third) and the top note (the fifth) a half step each. The intervals between the notes are both minor 3rds.

D Major Triad   **d diminished triad**

1. Write these triads.

d dim.   F Aug.   C Maj.   a♭ dim.   E♭ Maj.   g dim.

c♯ min.   a min.   E Aug.   B♭ Maj.   F♯ Maj.   b min.

2. Name these triads with their letter names and qualities (Major, minor, Augmented, or diminished). (The first one is done for you.)

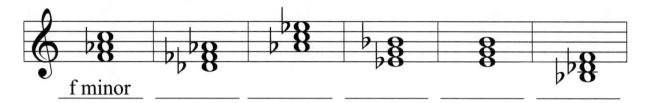

f minor _____ _____ _____ _____ _____

_____ _____ _____ _____ _____ _____

A **ROOT POSITION TRIAD** occurs when the note which names the triad is on the bottom. Root position triads are called 5/3 triads, because when the triad is in its simplest position, the intervals from the bottom note are a 5th and a 3rd. When labelling a triad in root position, only the letter name and quality are needed.

D Major Root Position Triad

A **FIRST INVERSION TRIAD** occurs when the **third** or **middle** note of the triad is the lowest note. First inversion triads are called 6/3 triads, because when they are in their simplest position (with the notes close together) they contain the intervals of a 6th and a 3rd above the bottom note.

When labelling first inversion triads, the symbol 6 (or $\frac{6}{3}$)is used beside the name of the triad.

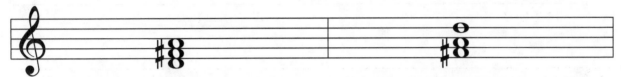

D Major Root Position Triad   D Major First Inversion Triad

(D Major ^{6})

A **SECOND INVERSION TRIAD** occurs when the **fifth** or **top** note of the triad is on the bottom. Second inversion triads are called 6/4 triads, because when they are in their simplest position (with the notes close together) they contain the intervals of a 6th and a 4th above the bottom note.

When labelling second inversion triads, the symbol $\frac{6}{4}$ is used beside the name of the triad.

D Major
Root Position Triad
(D Major)

D Major
First Inversion Triad
(D Major ^{6})

D Major
Second Inversion
Triad $\frac{6}{4}$
(D Major $\frac{6}{4}$)

3. Write these triads in root position, first inversion, and second inversion. (The first one is done for you.)

c minor

e♭ minor

A Major

F♯ Major

D Major

B Major

C♯ Major

a♭ minor

B♭ Major

g minor

E Major

f minor

4. Name these triads with their letter names, qualities, and inversions. (The first one is done for you.)

A Major $\frac{6}{4}$ ____ ____ ____ ____ ____

____ ____ ____ ____ ____ ____

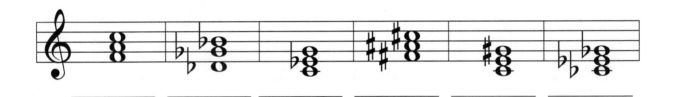

____ ____ ____ ____ ____ ____

5. Write these triads.

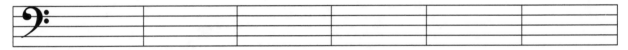

D♭ Maj. $\frac{6}{4}$ e min. 6   G♭ Maj. $\frac{6}{4}$ C♭ Maj. 6   A♭ Aug.   c♯ dim.

e♭ dim.   f♯ min. $\frac{6}{4}$ c dim.   d♭ dim.   c♭ min.   B Maj. $\frac{6}{4}$

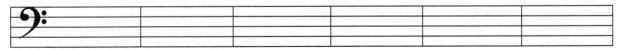

D Maj. $\frac{6}{4}$ f min. 6   F♯ Aug.   G Maj. 6   A Maj. $\frac{6}{4}$ B♭ Maj.

In actual music, triads are rarely in their simplest positions. To determine the letter name and quality of a triad within a piece, follow these steps:

a. Put the triad in its simplest form by placing the letter names so that there is one letter between each (for example, F-C-F-A becomes F-A-C).

b. Place all sharps or flats from the key signature, or from earlier in the measure, onto the letter names.

c. Determine the quality of the triad.

d. Determine the inversion of the triad by looking at the lowest note on the lowest staff.

Example (From *Minuet in G* by Beethoven):

a. Notes are B-D-D-G.

b. Simplest form is G-B-D.

c. G Major Triad.

d. B is the lowest note (in the bass clef), so the triad is in first inversion (6/3).

e. G Major ^{6} (or G Major $^6_3$)

6. Name the circled triads in the examples below by giving their letter names, qualitites, and inversions.

a. From *Polka* by Tchaikovsky.

_____ _____ _____ _____

b. From *Sailor's Song* by Grieg.

c. From *Sonatina, Op. 55, No. 3,* by Kuhlau.

LESSON 5
PRIMARY AND SECONDARY TRIADS

A triad can be built on each note of the scale.

When building triads on scale tones, all of the sharps or flats that are in the key being used must be added to the chords which have those notes.

Example: D Major Scale has F♯ and C♯. When writing the triads of D Major, every time an F or C appears in a chord, a sharp must be added to it. (See example below.)

Triads of the scale are numbered using Roman Numerals. Upper case Roman Numerals are used for Major triads, lower case Roman Numerals are used for minor triads, upper case Roman Numerals with a "+" are used for Augmented triads, and lower case Roman Numerals with "o" are used for diminished triads.

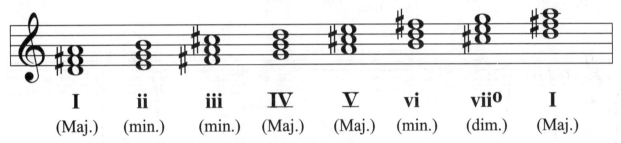

I	ii	iii	IV	V	vi	vii°	I
(Maj.)	(min.)	(min.)	(Maj.)	(Maj.)	(min.)	(dim.)	(Maj.)

I, IV, and V are the **PRIMARY TRIADS**. In Major keys, these three triads are Major, and are the most commonly used chords for harmonizing tonal melodies. The chords are labelled with upper case Roman Numerals.

ii, iii, vi, and vii° are the **SECONDARY TRIADS**. In Major keys, ii, iii, and vi are minor, and vii° is diminished. The chords are labelled with lower case Roman Numerals, and the vii° chord has a small circle beside the Roman Numeral.

The qualities of the triads in minor keys are different from those for Major keys. When using **harmonic minor**, the triads have the following qualities:

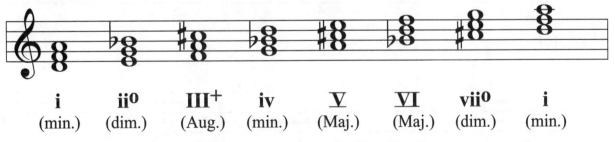

i	ii°	III⁺	iv	V	VI	vii°	i
(min.)	(dim.)	(Aug.)	(min.)	(Maj.)	(Maj.)	(dim.)	(min.)

PRIMARY AND SECONDARY TRIADS IN THE KEY OF D MINOR

1. Write the Primary and Secondary Triads for these keys, and label the triads with Roman Numerals. Circle each Primary Triad, and put a box around each Secondary Triad. Do not use a key signature. Write the sharps or flats before the notes. (The first one is done for you.)

I   ii   iii   IV   V   vi   vii°   I

E Major

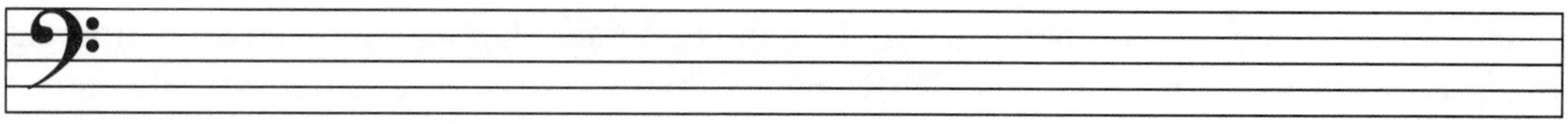

D♭ Major

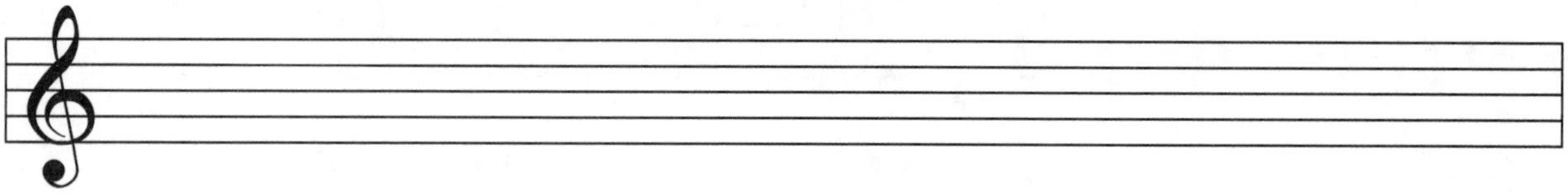

C Major

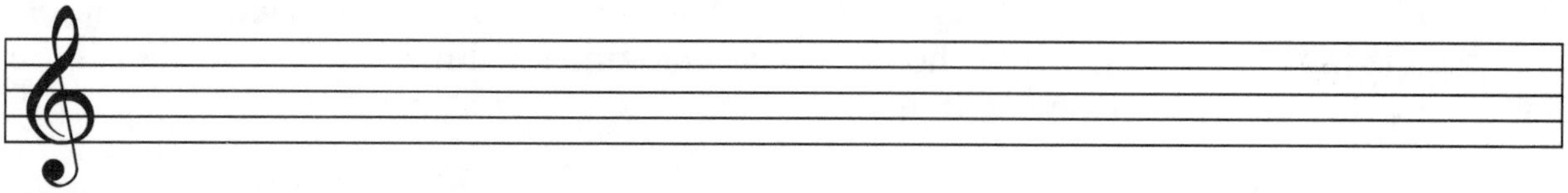

e minor

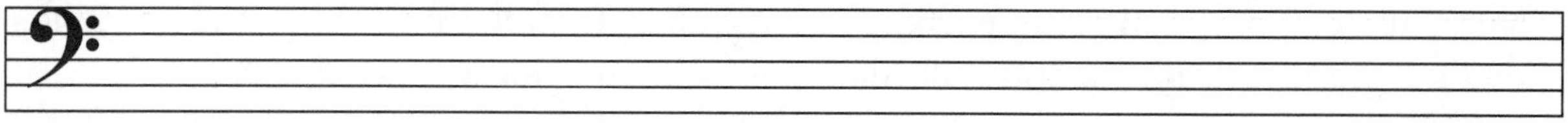

B Major

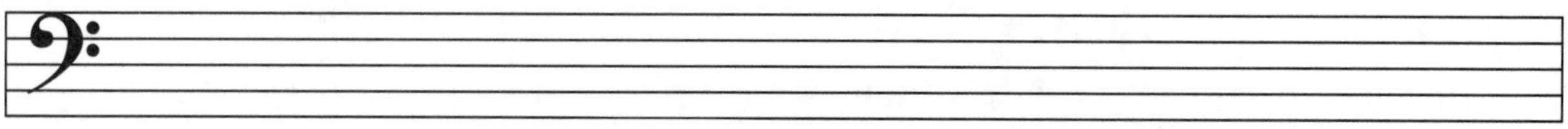

d minor

2. Write the Primary Triads for these keys, and label them with Roman Numerals. Do not use a key signature. Write the sharps or flats before the notes. (The first one is done for you.)

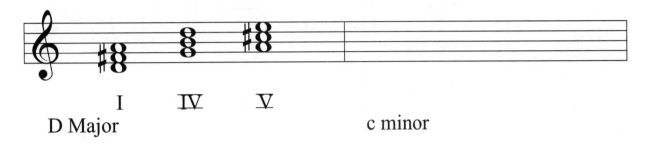

I IV V

D Major   c minor

C♯ Major   a minor

C♭ Major   d minor

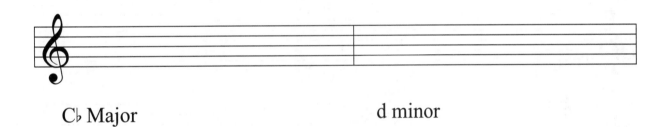

E♭ Major   b minor

Can you find the primary or secondary triads before they disappear?
Try PBJ's *Basics of Keyboard Theory Computer Activities, Levels 5-6.*
PBJ Music, 5062 Siesta Ln., Yorba Linda, CA, 92886, 714-961-0257, www.pbjmusic.com, teachme@pbjmusic.com

3. Write the Secondary Triads for these keys, and label them with Roman Numerals. Do not use a key signature. Write the sharps or flats before the notes. (The first one is done for you.)

    ii   iii   vi   viiº

D Major   F Major

b minor   A♭ Major

G♭ Major   F♯ Major

f minor   B♭ Major

Each degree of the scale has a name. These are called the **SCALE DEGREE NAMES:**

The **I** chord is **TONIC**.

The **ii** chord is **SUPERTONIC**.

The **iii** chord is **MEDIANT**.

The **IV** chord is **SUBDOMINANT**.

The **V** chord is **DOMINANT**.

The **vi** chord is **SUBMEDIANT**.

The **vii⁰** chord is **LEADING TONE**.

(Note: Qualities used above are from Major keys. The names stay the same when in minor.)

4. Match these Roman Numerals with their scale degree names.

a. ii   _____ Submediant

b. I   _____ Dominant

c. iii   _____ Supertonic

d. vii⁰   _____ Subdominant

e. IV   _____ Leading Tone

f. vi   _____ Mediant

g. V   _____ Tonic

5. Write the scale degree names for these Roman Numerals.

I   _____

ii   _____

iii   _____

IV   _____

V   _____

vi   _____

vii⁰   _____

In actual music, chords are rarely in their simplest position. To determine the Roman Numeral of a chord within a piece, do the following:

a.   Determine the Major or minor key of the piece.

b.   Put the chord in its simplest form by placing the letter names so that there is one letter between each (for example, F-C-F-A becomes F-A-C).

c.   Place all sharps or flats from the key signature or from earlier in the measure onto the letter names.

d.   Determine the Roman Numeral of the chord by counting from the letter name of the key up to the name of the chord.

e.   Determine the inversion of the chord by looking at the lowest note (on the lowest staff).

Example (From *Minuet in G* by Beethoven):

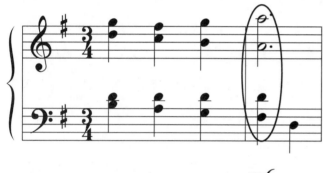

$\underline{V}^6$

a.   Key of G Major

b.   Notes are: F#-D-A-A

c.   Simplest form is: D-F#-A

d.   D Major Triad. The piece is in the key of G Major. D is the fifth note of the G Major Scale; therefore, this is the V chord.

e.   The lowest note (in the bass clef) is F#. The chord is in first inversion. Label the chord $\underline{V}$6/3, or $\underline{V}^6$ as an abbreviation.

6. Label the circled chords below. Put the Roman Numeral and inversion for each.

a. From *Folk Song* by Schumann.   Key of: _____

_____   _____ _____ _____ _____

b. From *Ecossaise No. 1, K. WoO83*, by Beethoven. Key of: _____

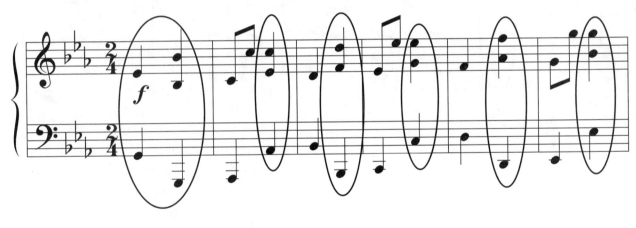

_____   _____   _____   _____   _____   _____

c. From *Sonatina, Op. 36, No. 5*, by Clementi. Key of: _____

_____   _____   _____   _____

d. From *Sonatina, Op. 36, No. 6,* by Clementi. Key of: _____

e. From *Polka* by Tchaikovsky. Key of: _____

LESSON 6
THE DOMINANT SEVENTH CHORD

The **<u>DOMINANT SEVENTH CHORD</u>** is created by adding a note to a Major triad which is a minor seventh above the root of the triad. The Dominant Seventh chord has four different notes.

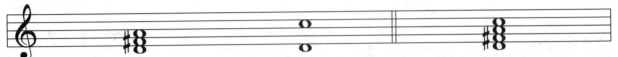

**D MAJOR TRIAD   MINOR 7TH (m7)   DOMINANT SEVENTH
CHORD ON D**

Inversions of the Dominant 7th are as follows:

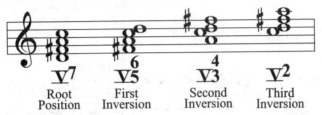

V^7 $\quad$ V^6_5 $\quad$ V^4_3 $\quad$ V^2

Root $\quad$ First $\quad$ Second $\quad$ Third
Position $\quad$ Inversion $\quad$ Inversion $\quad$ Inversion

The Dominant Seventh is so named because it is based on the V or Dominant chord, and has the interval of a 7th within the chord.

Dominant Seventh chords can be on a given note, or in a given key. When asked to write a Dominant Seventh on a given note, write a Major triad with an added minor seventh.

DOMINANT SEVENTH (DOM. 7) ON D

When asked to write a Dominant Seventh in a given key, find the V chord for that key, and add a note which is a minor seventh above the root. In Major keys, no accidentals will be added to the chord.

DOMINANT 7TH IN THE KEY OF D MAJOR

In minor keys, the third of the chord must be raised with an accidental, because harmonic minor is used.

DOMINANT 7TH IN THE KEY OF G MINOR

1. Write Dominant Seventh chords and their inversions in the following keys, and label the chords with Roman Numerals. Be sure to use harmonic minor. The first one is given.

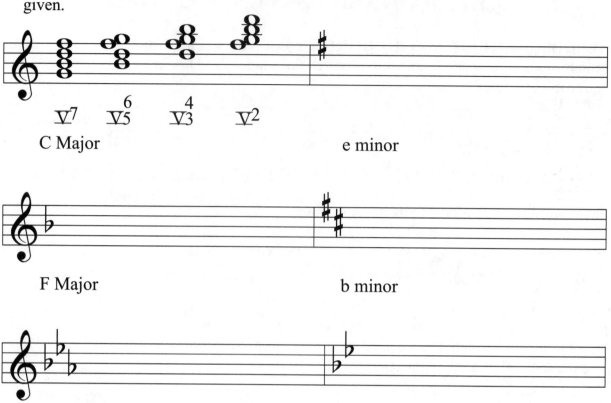

C Major   e minor

F Major   b minor

Eb Major   g minor

2. Complete Dominant 7th chords and their inversions on these notes. Use accidentals before the notes. Do not use a key signature.

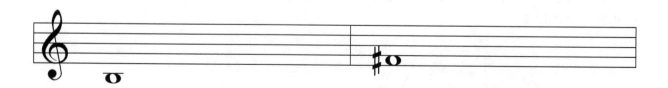

3. Label the circled chords in the examples below with their Roman Numerals and inversions. Some are V chords and some are V7 chords (or their inversions). (The first one is done for you.)

a. Beethoven: *Für Elise*

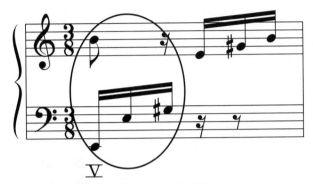

V

b. Tchaikovsky: *Polka*

_____

c. Scarlatti: *Sonata, L. 58*

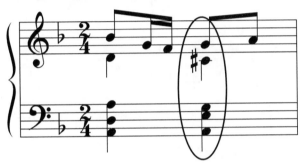

_____

d. Beethoven: *Bagatelle, Op. 119, No. 2*

_____

e. Kuhlau: *Sonatina, Op. 55, No. 1*

_____

f. Kuhlau: *Sonatina, Op. 55, No. 3*

_____

g. Schumann: *Norse Song*

_____

h. Beethoven: *Für Elise*

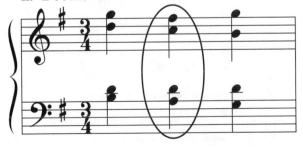

_____

i. Schumann: *Folk Song*

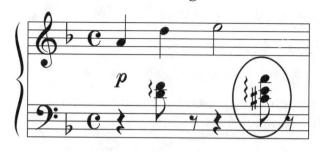

___

j. Schumann: *Folk Song*

___

k. Clementi: *Sonatina, Op. 36, No. 5*

___

l. Clementi: *Sonatina, Op. 36, No. 6*

___

m. Schumann: *Album for the Young,*
No. 21 (Untitled)

___

n. Schumann: *Norse Song*

___

o. Beethoven: *Joyful, Sorrowful*

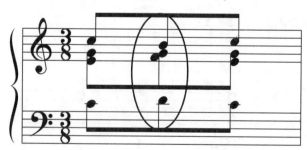

___

p. Beethoven: *Minuet in D*

___

LESSON 7
AUTHENTIC, HALF, PLAGAL,
AND DECEPTIVE CADENCES

A **CADENCE** is a closing or ending for a musical phrase, made up of a combination of chords. There are many types of cadences. Four common cadences are:

AUTHENTIC, HALF, PLAGAL, and DECEPTIVE CADENCES

An **AUTHENTIC CADENCE** consists of a V or V^7 chord followed by a I chord:

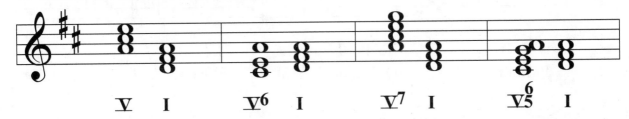

1. Write Authentic Cadences in these keys, using the chords indicated by the Roman Numerals. (The first one is given.) Be sure to use harmonic minor.

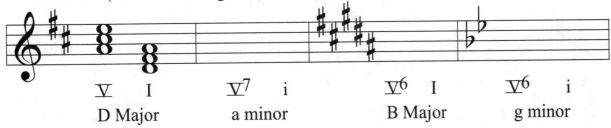

A **PLAGAL CADENCE** consists of a IV chord followed by a I chord:

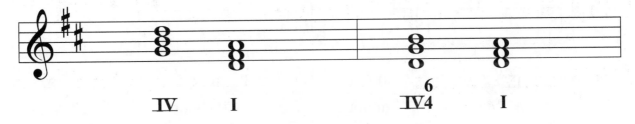

2. Write Plagal Cadences in these keys, using the chords indicated by the Roman Numerals. (The first one is given.)

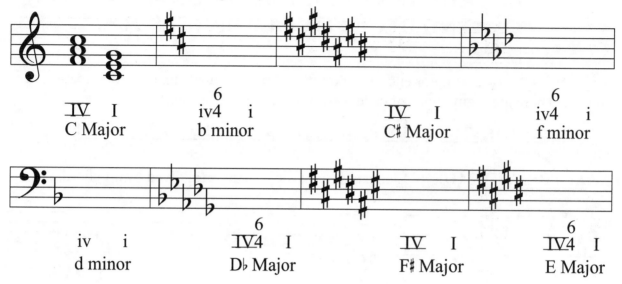

A **HALF CADENCE** is a cadence which ends with a V or V⁷ chord:

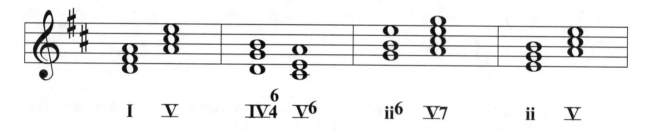

3. Write Half Cadences in these keys, using the chords indicated by the Roman Numerals. (The first one is given.) Be sure to use harmonic minor.

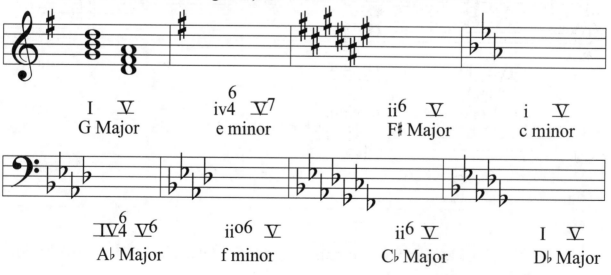

A **DECEPTIVE CADENCE** consists of a V (or sometimes IV) chord followed by a vi chord:

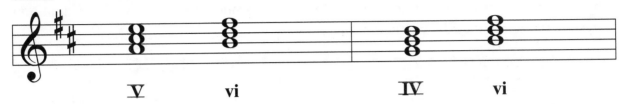

<u>V</u>   **vi**   <u>IV</u>   **vi**

4. Write Deceptive Cadences in these keys, using the chords indicated by the Roman Numerals. (The first one is given.)

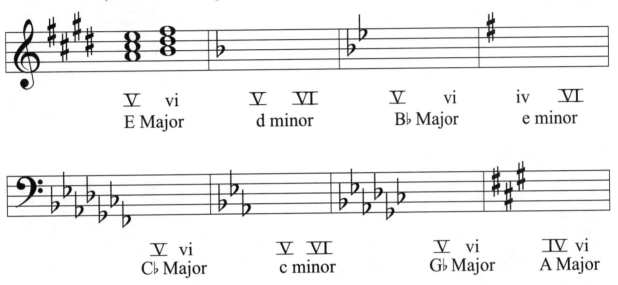

<u>V</u> vi   <u>V</u> <u>VI</u>   <u>V</u> vi   iv <u>VI</u>
E Major   d minor   B♭ Major   e minor

<u>V</u> vi   <u>V</u> <u>VI</u>   <u>V</u> vi   <u>IV</u> vi
C♭ Major   c minor   G♭ Major   A Major

5. Label the chords of each of these cadences with Roman Numerals and inversion numbers, then put the type of cadence (Authentic, Half, Plagal, or Deceptive) on the line below the Roman Numerals. (The first one is given.)

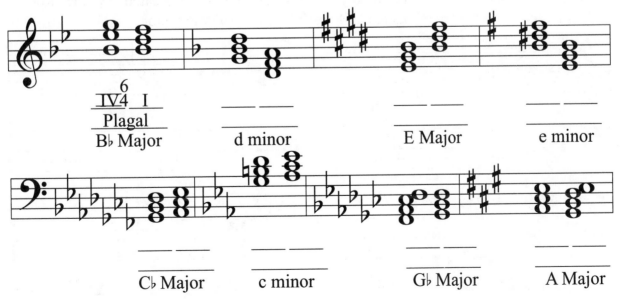

<u>IV$^6_4$</u> I   ____ ____   ____ ____   ____ ____
<u>Plagal</u>
B♭ Major   d minor   E Major   e minor

____ ____   ____ ____   ____ ____   ____ ____

C♭ Major   c minor   G♭ Major   A Major

A **CHORD PROGRESSION** or **MIXED CADENCE** is created by a series of four or five primary triads, using inversions for some of the triads. **Common tones** are used when moving from one chord to another, to create a smooth progression. The common tones are circled in the first example below.

6. Write these chord progressions. The first one is given.

When labelling cadences in music literature, label the last two chords of the phrase with their Roman Numerals. These are the two chords which make up the cadence. Then, give the cadence its name (Authentic, Half, Plagal, or Deceptive).

Example: From *Sonatina, Op. 36, No. 4*, by Clementi:

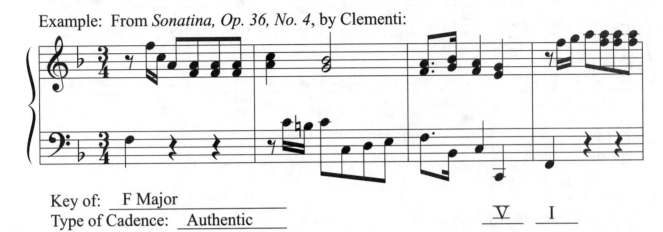

Key of: __F Major__

Type of Cadence: __Authentic__   V   I

7. Name the cadence at the end of each phrase of music below. Give the name of the Major or minor key, write the Roman Numerals for the last two chords, then write the type of cadence (Authentic, Half, or Plagal).

   a. From *Sonatina, Op. 36, No. 6*, by Clementi.

Key of: _____

Type of Cadence: _____   ____ ____

   b. From *Echos from the Theatre* by Schumann.

Key of: _____

Type of Cadence: _____   ____   ____

c. From *Ecossaise, K. Wo0 83* by Beethoven.

Key of: _____

Type of Cadence: _____   _____   _____

d. From *Baba-Yaga* by Tchaikovsky.

Key of: _____

Type of Cadence: _____   _____   _____

e. From *Sonatina, Hob. XVI: 8*, by Haydn.

Key of: _____

Type of Cadence: _____   _____   _____

f. From *Albumleaf, Op. Posth.*, by Chopin.

Key of: _____

Type of Cadence: _____   _____   _____

g. From *Minuet in G* by Beethoven.

Key of: _____

Type of Cadence: _____   _____   _____

h. From *Sonatina, Op. 55, No. 1*, by Kuhlau.

Key of: _____

Type of Cadence: _____   _____   _____

i. From *Norse Song* by Schumann.

Key of: _____

Type of Cadence: _____ ____ ____

j. From *Folk Song* by Schumann.

Key of: _____

Type of Cadence: _____ ____ ____

REVIEW
WORDS USED IN LESSONS 1-7

Authentic Cadence: A V-I cadence (in harmomic minor, V-i).

Cadence: A closing or ending for a phrase of music, made up of two or more chords.

Chromatic Scale: A scale containing all twelve notes, with half-steps between all notes.

Dominant Seventh: A four note chord made up of a Major triad, and a minor 7th above the root. Root position is V^7, first inversion is V 6/5, second inversion is V 4/3, and third inversion is V^2.

First Inversion: A triad written with the third as the lowest note.

Half Cadence: A cadence which ends with the V chord.

Interval: The distance between two notes, named with numbers.

Inversion: A triad written in a position in which the note that names the triad is not the lowest.

Key Signature: The sharps or flats at the beginning of a piece of music. (There are Major and minor key signatures.)

Plagal Cadence: A IV-I cadence (in harmonic minor, iv-i).

Primary Triads: The I, IV, and V chords. (In minor, i, iv, and V.)

Root Position: A traid written in a position so that the note which names it is the lowest.

Scale: A series of notes in alphabetical order (for example, C-D-E-F-G-A-B-C).

Scale Degree Names: Tonic (I), Supertonic (ii), Mediant (iii), Subdominant (IV), Dominant (V), Submediant (vi), Leading Tone (vii^o).

Second Inversion: A triad written with the fifth as the lowest note.

Secondary Triads: the ii, iii, vi, and vii^o chords. (In harmonic minor, ii^o, III$^+$, VI, and vii^o).

Triad: A chord with three different notes in it.   Qualities may   be Major, minor, Augmented, or diminished.

REVIEW
LESSONS 1-7

1. Name these Major keys.

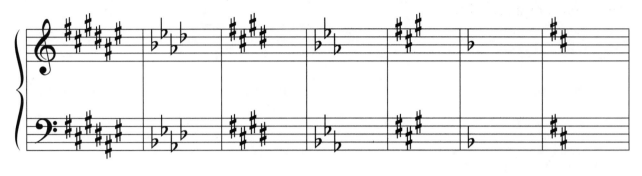

___ ___ ___ ___ ___ ___ ___

2. Name these <u>minor</u> keys.

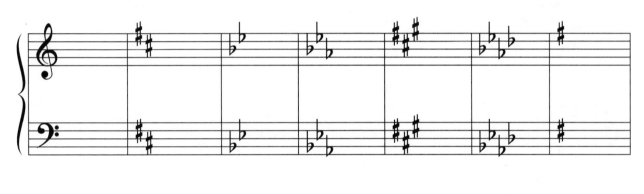

___ ___ ___ ___ ___ ___ ___

3. Write the key signatures for these keys, in both clefs.

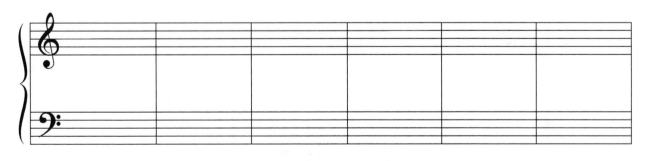

   C♯ Major   B♭ Major   c minor   f minor   D♭ Major   e minor

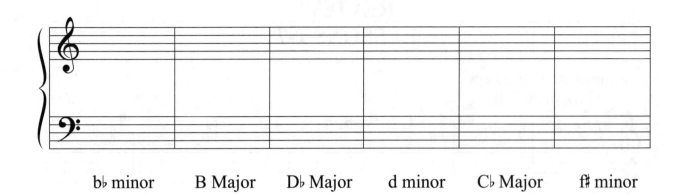

b♭ minor   B Major   D♭ Major   d minor   C♭ Major   f♯ minor

4. Write these scales.

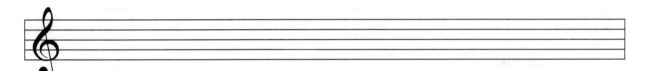

Chromatic Scale beginning on E

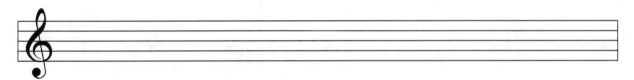

c harmonic minor

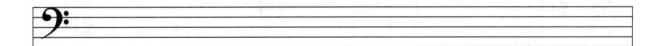

f♯ harmonic minor

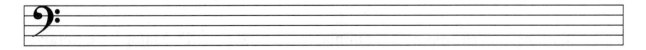

G♭ Major

bb natural minor

g harmonic minor

C# Major

Db Major

5. Label these triads with their letter names, qualities, (Major, minor, Augmented, or diminished), and inversions. (The first one is done for you.)

E Major 6 _____ _____ _____ _____ _____

_____ _____ _____ _____ _____

6. Write these triads.

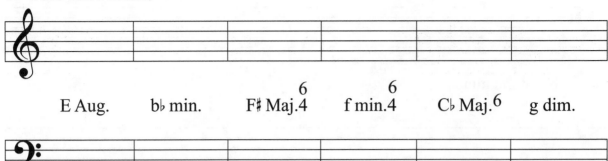

E Aug.   b♭ min.   F♯ Maj.⁶₄   f min.⁶₄   C♭ Maj.⁶   g dim.

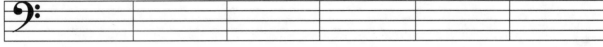

d dim.   e dim.   B♭ Aug.   a min.⁶   A Aug.   F Maj.⁶

7. Name these intervals. The first one is given.

P4

8. Complete these intervals. Do not change the given note. The first one is given.

A3 up   A7 down   m2 up   P4 down   P5 down   d8 up   A4 down   A6 down

9. Write Dominant Seventh chords in these keys. The first one is given.

E♭ Major   a minor   A Major   e minor   E Major   d minor

10. Complete Dominant Seventh chords on these notes.

11. Name the Major key to which each of these Dominant Sevenths belongs.

_____ _____ _____ _____ _____ _____

12. Write the scale degree names for the following Roman Numerals.

I or i _____

ii or ii⁰ _____

iii or III⁺ _____

IV or iv _____

V _____

vi or VI _____

vii⁰ _____

13. Write these chord progressions.

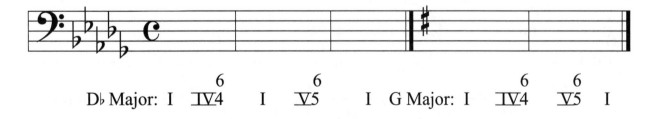

D♭ Major: I   IV⁶₄   I   V⁶₅   I   G Major: I   IV⁶₄   V⁶₅   I

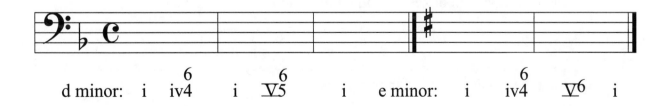

d minor: i   iv⁶₄   i   V⁶₅   i   e minor: i   iv⁶₄   V⁶   i

14. The following example is from *Bagatelle, Op. 119, No. 1*, by Beethoven. Answer the questions about the music.

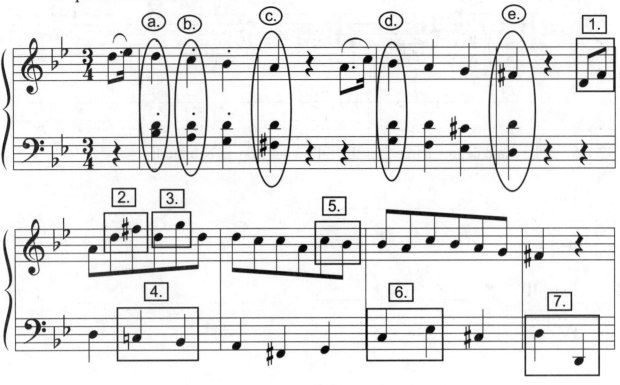

a. What is the key or tonality? _____ _____

b. Which form of minor is used? _____

c. Give the letter name, quality, Roman Numeral, and inversion for each circled chord. (The first one is given.)

	LETTER	QUALITY	ROMAN NUMERAL & INVERSION
Triad a.	g	minor	i⁶
Triad b.			
Triad c.			
Triad d.			
Triad e.			

d. Name the intervals with boxes around them. The first one is given.

1. __M3__   2. _____   3. _____   4. _____   5. _____   6. _____   7. _____

e. Name the type of cadence used in measures 7-8. _____

15. The following example is from a Waltz by Schubert. Answer the questions about the music.

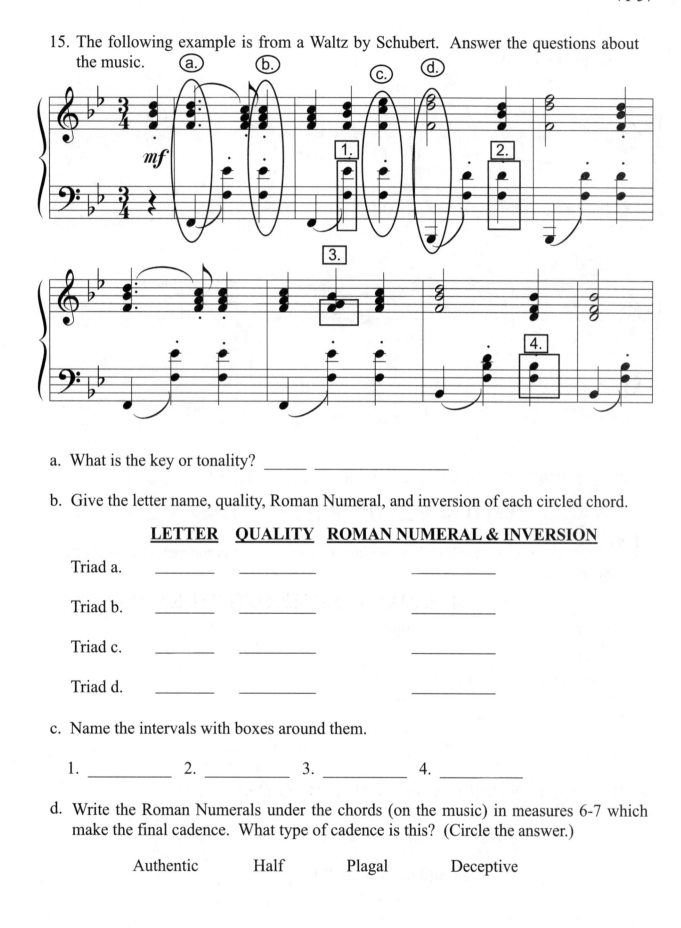

a. What is the key or tonality? _____ _____

b. Give the letter name, quality, Roman Numeral, and inversion of each circled chord.

LETTER   QUALITY   ROMAN NUMERAL & INVERSION

Triad a.   _____   _____   _____

Triad b.   _____   _____   _____

Triad c.   _____   _____   _____

Triad d.   _____   _____   _____

c. Name the intervals with boxes around them.

1. _____   2. _____   3. _____   4. _____

d. Write the Roman Numerals under the chords (on the music) in measures 6-7 which make the final cadence. What type of cadence is this? (Circle the answer.)

Authentic   Half   Plagal   Deceptive

16. The following example is from Sonatina, Op. 55, No. 3, by Kuhlau. Answer the questions about the music.

a. What is the key or tonality? _____ _____

b. Give the letter name, quality, Roman Numeral, and inversion for each circled chord.

	LETTER	**QUALITY**	**ROMAN NUMERAL & INVERSION**
Triad a.	_____	_____	_____
Triad b.	_____	_____	_____
Triad c.	_____	_____	_____
Triad d.	_____	_____	_____

c. Name the intervals with boxes around them.

1. _____   2. _____   3. _____   4. _____   5. _____   6. _____   7. _____

d. What type of cadence is used at the end of measure 4? _____

e. Write the secondary triads for this key on the staff below, and label the triads with Roman Numerals.

LESSON 8
TIME SIGNATURES

The **TIME SIGNATURE** for a piece of music is found at the beginning, next to the key signature. The time signature is made up of two numbers:

Sometimes, the letter $\mathbf{C}$ or $\mathbf{\cancel{C}}$ is used instead of numbers.

$\mathbf{C}$ stands for $\dfrac{4}{4}$, or **Common Time.**

$\mathbf{\cancel{C}}$ stands for $\dfrac{2}{2}$, or **Alla Breve.**

The **top** number of the time signature tells **how many beats each measure contains.**

The **bottom** number tells **which type of note receives one beat.**

     2 = 2 beats or counts per measure
     4 = Quarter note (♩) receives one beat

     3 = 3 beats or counts per measure
     8 = Eighth note (♪) receives one beat

METER is the number of equal beats per measure.

When the bottom number of a time signature is a "4," a quarter note (♩) receives one beat or count. The following chart shows how many beats to give these notes or rests:

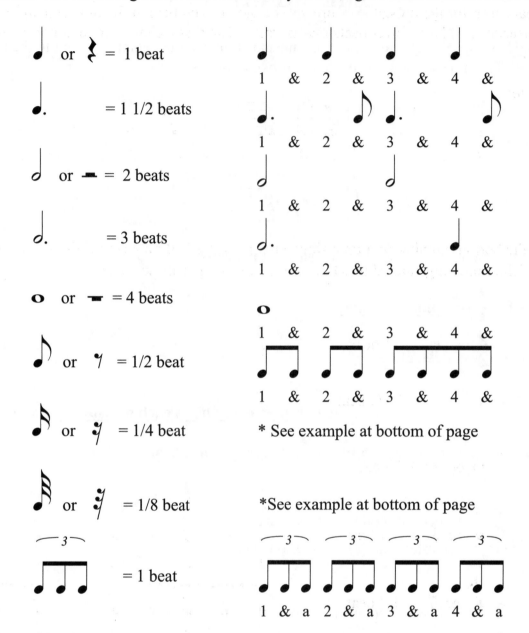

♩ or 𝄽 = 1 beat

♩. = 1 1/2 beats

♩ or ▬ = 2 beats

♩. = 3 beats

o or ▬ = 4 beats

♪ or 𝄾 = 1/2 beat

♬ or 𝄿 = 1/4 beat

♬ or 𝅀 = 1/8 beat

⌐3¬
♫♫ = 1 beat

* See example at bottom of page

*See example at bottom of page

* Counting for some of the more common eighth, sixteenth, and thirty-second note patterns is shown here:

1 e & a 2 & a 3& a 4 e &   1 e & a 2 e & a 3e &a 4 e &

An **UPBEAT** occurs when an incomplete measure begins the piece. The last beat or beats are "borrowed" from the final measure of the piece and placed at the beginning. The beats used for the upbeat measure will be the last numbers of the time signature. The final measure will have fewer beats than normal. The first full measure begins with count number 1.

Example:

4   &   1   &   2   &   3   &   4   &   1   &   2   &   3   &

When the bottom number of a time signature is a "2," a half note (♩) receives one beat or count. The following chart shows how many beats to give these notes or rests:

♩ or ▬ = 1 beat

♩. = 1 1/2 beats

𝅝 or ▬ = 2 beats

♩ or 𝄽 = 1/2 beat

♪ or 𝄾 = 1/4 beat

♫ or 𝄿 = 1/8 beat

♬ or 𝅀 = 1/16 beat

When the time signature for a piece of music has an 8 on the bottom, an eighth note (♪) receives one beat.

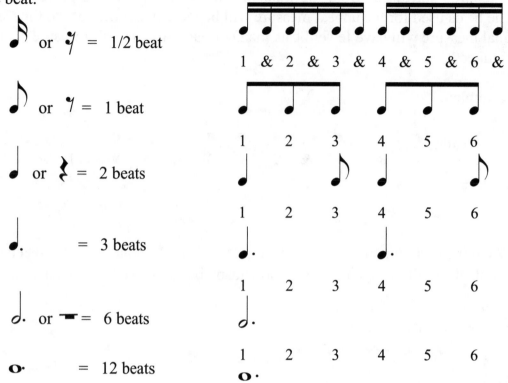

♪ or 𝄿 = 1/2 beat

♪ or 𝄾 = 1 beat

♩ or 𝄽 = 2 beats

♩. = 3 beats

♩. or ▬ = 6 beats

𝅝. = 12 beats

1. Fill in the blanks. (The first one is done for you.)

$\frac{2}{4}$ = <u>2 beats per measure</u>
= <u>Quarter note receives one beat or count</u>

$\frac{3}{4}$ = _____
= _____

$\frac{3}{8}$ = _____
= _____

C = _____

₵ = _____

$\frac{2}{2}$ = _____
= _____

$\frac{7}{4}$ = _____
= _____

$\frac{6}{8}$ = _____
= _____

When a time signature has a 2 on top (2/2, 2/4, etc.), the first beat of the measure is strongest.

When a time signature has a 3 on top (3/8, 3/4, etc.), the first beat of the measure is strongest.

When a time signature has a 4 on top (4/2, 4/4, etc.), the first beat of the measure is strongest, and the third beat is also a strong beat.

When a time signature has a 6 on top (6/8, 6/4, etc.), the first beat of the measure is strongest, and the fourth beat is also a strong beat.

Note: The accents above are only intended to demonstrate where strong and weak beats occur within the given meter. They are not meant to imply that every strong beat receives an accent.

2. Write the counts for these phrases, and place accents on the strong beats.   (The first measure is given.)

a. From *Sonatina, Op. 36, No. 4,* by Clementi.

b. From *Sonatina, Op. 36, No. 5*, by Clementi.

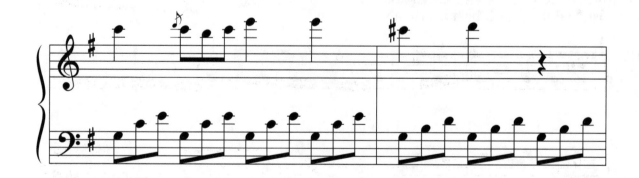

c. From *Sonatina, Op. 36, No. 6,* by Clementi.

d. From *Für Elise* by Beethoven.

e. From *Echoes from the Theatre* by Schumann.

f. From *Baba Yaga* by Tchaikovsky.

g. From *March* by Prokofiev.

h. From *Pleasantry II* by Bartok.

LESSON 9
SIGNS AND TERMS

Music often contains signs and terms other than notes and rhythms. Memorize the ones listed below.

A Tempo: Return to the original tempo (the speed at which the piece began).

 Accent: Play the note louder than the others.

Accelerando: Accelerate; gradually faster.

Accidentals: Sharps, flats, or naturals written before the notes (not in the key signature).

Adagio: Slowly.

Allegro: Fast or quick.

Allegretto: Slighly slower than Allegro; faster than Andante.

Andante: A moderate walking tempo.
                    Andante.)
Andantino: Slightly faster than Andante. (Some composers use it to mean slower than

Animato: Animated; with spirit.

 **Appoggiatura:** Used mainly in music of the Classical Period (see Lesson 14), play the first note as half the value of the second note:

Arpeggio: A continuous broken chord:

Cantabile: In a singing style.

Con Brio: With vigor or spirit (with brilliance).

Con Moto: With motion.

Crescendo: Gradually louder.

D.C. al Fine: Go back to the beginning of the piece, and play until the word *Fine* (which means end).

𝄻 ❋ or |_____| **Damper Pedal:** Press the pedal located on the right.

⬎ **Decrescendo:** Gradually softer.

Dolce: Sweetly.

Doloroso: Sadly; sorrowfully.

Double Flat: Two flats placed before a note, indicating to lower the note a whole step.

B double flat is
played as A on
the piano

Double Sharp: The symbol 𝄪 placed before a note, indicating to raise the note a whole step.

G double sharp is
played as A on
the piano.

Dynamics: Letters or symbols which tell how loudly or softly to play the music.

Enharmonic: Two different names for the same pitch, such as C♯ and D♭.

Espressivo: Expressively.

𝆑 **Forte:** Loud.

𝆑𝆑 **Fortissimo:** Very loud.

𝆑𝆑𝆑 **Fortississimo:** Very, very loud.

𝆑𝆏 **Forte-piano:** Loud followed immediately by soft.

⌒ **Fermata:** Hold the note longer than its value.

First and Second Ending: Play the piece with the first ending (under the 1.), then repeat the piece. The second time through, skip the first ending and play the second ending (under the 2.).

Largo: Very slowly; "large."

Legato Sign (slur): Play smoothly; connect the notes.

Leggiero: lightly, delicately.

Lento: Slowly.

Marcato: Stressed, marked.

mf **Mezzo Forte:** Medium loud.

mp **Mezzo Piano:** Medium soft.

Moderato: A moderate or medium tempo.

Molto: Much; very.

 **Mordent:** An ornament in which the written note is played, followed by the note below the written note and the written note again:

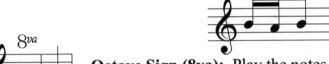

Octave Sign (8va): Play the notes an octave higher (or lower if below the notes) than where they are written.

Opus: A word used to indicate the chronological order in which a composer's music was written.

Ostinato: A repeated pattern, such as:

Parallel Major/minor: Major and minor keys with the same letter names (such as C Major and c minor).

p **Piano:** Soft.

pp **Pianissimo:** Very soft.

ppp **Pianississimo:** Very, very soft.

Phrase: A musical sentence, often four measures long.

Presto: Very fast.

Poco: Little.

Rallentando: Gradually slower.

Repeat Sign: Repeat the previous sections of music. Go back to the nearest repeat sign, or to the beginning of the piece if there is none.

Ritardando (*ritard., rit.,*): Slow down gradually.

Robusto: Robustly, boldly.

Scherzando: Playfully, jokingly.

sf fz sfz   Sforzando: A sudden, sharp accent.

Simile: Continue in the same style.

 Slur: Connect the first note to the second, then release the second note.

Spiritoso: Spirited; with spirit.

Sostenuto: Sustained.

 **Staccato:** Play crisply or detached.

Subito: Suddenly; at once.

Syncopation: A momentary contradiction of the meter or pulse, often by changing strong and weak beats within a measure. For example:

Tempo: The speed at which to play the music.

Tenuto or Stress: Play the note slightly louder than the others; stress the note. May also mean to give the note its full value.

Tranquillo: Tranquilly, peacefully, calmly.

Tre Corda: Release the Una Corda pedal (soft pedal; left pedal).

Trill: An ornament in which the written note is alternated continuously with the note above. In music of the Baroque or Classical Period (see Lessons 13 and 14), begin the trill on the note above the written note (example A). In music of the Romantic Period (Lesson 15), begin on the written note (example B).

Example A:
Baroque or
Classical.

Example B:
Romantic.

Turn: An ornament in which the written note is surrounded by its upper and lower neighbors:

Una Corda: Often abbreviated U.C. in music. Press the left or soft pedal.

Vivace: Quick, lively.

Vivo: Brisk, lively.

1. Match these terms and symbols with their definitions.

_____	*p*	a. Mezzo Piano: Meduim soft
_____	*mf*	b. Pianissimo: Very soft
_____	*sfz*	c. Piano: Soft
_____	*mp*	d. Fortissimo: Very loud
_____	*ppp*	e. Mezzo Forte: Medium loud
_____	*fff*	f. Symbols that indicate loud or soft
_____	Dynamics	g. Forte: Loud
_____	*ff*	h. Play one octave higher
_____	8*va*	i. Fortississimo: Very, very loud
_____	*f*	j. Sforzando: A sudden, sharp accent
_____	*pp*	k. Pianississimo: Very, very soft

2. Match these terms and symbols with their definitions.

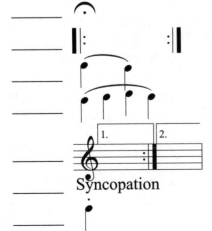

a. Legato: Connect the notes

b. Repeat the music

c. Strong notes on weak beats

d. Slur: Connect the first note to the second note

e. Fermata: Hold the note longer

f. First and Second Ending

g. Staccato: Detached

3. Match these terms and symbols with their definitions.

_____ 𝅗𝅥 (tenuto note)   a. Use the damper pedal (the pedal on the right)

_____ 𝅗𝅥 (accent note)   b. A musical sentence, often four measures long

_____ Phrase   c. Stress or tenuto: Stress the note, or play it slightly
                                      louder than the others

_____ Ped. ✽ |_____| d. Accent: Play the note louder than the others

_____ D. C. al Fine   e. Slow down gradually

_____ Ritardando (*rit.*)   f. Return to the original tempo (the speed with which
                                      you began the music)

_____ A Tempo   g. Go back to the beginning and play until you see the
                                      word "*Fine*"

4. Match these terms and symbols with their definitions.

_____ Allegro   a. A moderate walking tempo

_____ Andante   b. Gradually louder

_____ Moderato   c. Slow down gradually

_____ Vivace   d. Gradually softer

_____ ⟨crescendo⟩   e. Slowly

_____ ⟨decrescendo⟩   f. A moderate or medium tempo

_____ Adagio   g. Quick or lively

_____ Lento   h. With brilliance

_____ Rallentando   i. Fast, quick

_____ Con Brio   j. Slowly

5. Match these terms and symbols with their definitions.

_____ Sostenuto

_____ Scherzando

_____ Doloroso

_____ Opus

_____ Robusto

_____ ***fp***

a. Sadly, sorrowfully

b. Boldly, robustly

c. Loud, followed immediately by soft

d. Sustained

e. Playfully, jokingly

f. System of classifying a composer's music chronologically

6. Match these terms and symbols with their definitions.

_____ Presto

_____ Vivo

_____ Espressivo

_____ Leggiero

_____ Tranquillo

_____ Allegretto

_____ Subito

_____ Animato

_____ Largo

a. Expressively

b. Tranquilly, peacefully

c. Suddenly; at once

d. Very fast

e. Very slowly; "large"

f. Brisk, lively

g. Slightly slower than Allegro

h. Lightly; delicately

i. Animated; with spirit

7. Match these terms and symbols with their definitions.

_____ Andantino

_____ Con Moto

_____ Dolce

_____

_____ Accelerando

_____ (Baroque & Classical Periods)

_____ Una Corda

_____ Cantabile

_____ Molto

_____

_____ (Romantic Period)

_____

_____ Poco

_____ Tre Corde

_____ Spiritoso

_____ Arpeggio

_____ Ostinato

_____

_____

_____ Accidental

a. Trill:

b. Gradually faster

c. Turn:

d. Use soft pedal (left pedal)

e. Slightly faster than Andante

f. Sweetly

g. With motion

h. With spirit

i. Little

j. Much; greatly

k. Appoggiatura:

l. Release the soft pedal (left pedal)

m. Trill:

n. In a singing style

o. Mordent:

p. Double flat

q. A repeated pattern

r. A continuous broken chord

s. Double sharp

t. Sharp, flat, or natural written before the note (not in the key signature)

LESSON 10
MOTIVE; REPETITION, IMITATION, SEQUENCE

A **MOTIVE** (or motif) is a short group of notes used in a piece of music. The composer uses this motive as the main idea of the music and repeats it in many different ways.

A **THEME** is an entire phrase of music, which is the basis of the composition. (A composition may have more than one theme.)

Beethoven's *Symphony No. 5* uses this motive:

It is repeated, with variations, several times at the beginning of the symphony:

This motive is used often throughout the symphony. It would be helpful to listen to the entire first movement of Beethoven's *Symphony No. 5*, and you will hear this motif used in many interesting ways.

REPETITION takes place when the motive is repeated immediately, exactly the way it was the first time it occurred, on the same note.

Short Prelude No. 3 by J.S. Bach uses repetition. The repetition is circled.

SEQUENCE occurs when the motive is repeated immediately, on a different note, usually a 2nd or 3rd higher or lower.

Short Prelude No. 8 by J.S. Bach uses sequence. The sequences in the example below are circled.

IMITATION occurs when the motive is repeated immediately in another voice, such as in the bass clef following a statement of the motive in the treble clef.

Short Prelude No. 8 by J.S. Bach uses imitation. The imitation is circled.

1. Circle the Repetition, Imitation, or Sequence in each example below, then write the type of technique (Repetition, Imitation, or Sequence) on the line above the music.

a. From *Little Prelude No. 1* by J.S. Bach. _____

b. From *Puck* by Grieg. _____

c. From *Waltz in B♭* by Schubert. _____

d. From *Little Prelude No. 2* by J.S. Bach. _____

e. From *Little Prelude No. 6* by J.S. Bach. _____

f. From *Revelry* by Bartok. _____

g. From *Little Prelude No. 7* by J.S. Bach. _____

LESSON 11
TRANSPOSITION

TRANSPOSITION occurs when a piece of music is played or written in a key that is different from the original.

For example, the first version of "Frere Jacques" below (Example A) is in the key of C Major. The second version (Example B) is in G Major. The piece has been transposed from C Major to G Major.

Notice how the intervals remain the same in both versions, and if played, the melody sounds the same, but higher in pitch.

EXAMPLE A: FRERE JACQUES in the key of C Major

EXAMPLE B: FRERE JACQUES in the key of G Major

Follow these steps when transposing a melody:

1. Determine the key of the original melody.

2. Determine the key signature of the key to which the music will be transposed.

3. Look at the first note of the original melody and determine its scale degree or its place in the scale. For example, if the original key is C Major and the melody begins on G, the starting note is the 5th.

4. The first note for the new key will be the same interval above the new tonic as the original. For example, when the new key is D Major and the starting note was a 5th above tonic, the newstarting note will be A, a 5th above D.

5. Continue writing the transposition by determining each interval of the original melody and using that interval for the new melody. Add any necessary sharps or flats.

6. Check your progress by following steps 3 and 4 for any given note.

Example: Mary Had a Little Lamb, transposed from C Major to G Major.

1. Original key: C Major.
2. New key signature for G Major: F#.
3. First note of original is E, the 3rd note of G Major
4. Starting note will be B, the 3rd note of G Major.
5. Melody moves up and down by seconds and thirds.

MARY HAD A LITTLE LAMB in C Major

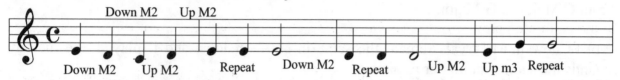

MARY HAD A LITTLE LAMB in G Major

Another way to transpose a melody is to move each note up or down the same distance. In the example of "Mary Had a Little Lamb" above, each note would be moved up a Perfect 5th from the original. The first E becomes B, the D becomes A, the C becomes G, etc.

1. Transpose these melodies to the given key. Write the transposition on the blank staff.

a. Transpose to Bb Major

b. Transpose to a minor

LESSON 12
MODULATION

MODULATION occurs when a musical compsition changes from the original key to another key, and remains in the new key for a reasonable amount of time.

A piece of music may modulate to any other key, but frequently either the Dominant (V) key or the relative Major or minor is used.

In the example below, from *Sonatina, Op. 55, No. 1*, by Kuhlau, the music begins in the key of C Major, and modulates to the key of G Major.

Two important 20th Century theorists, Schoenberg and Schenker, taught that music does not truly modulate, but that sections of music which appear to modulate are essentially extended cadences, and that these sections are not much different in essence from sections which use any chord other than tonic.

1. Tell the name of the key to which each of these excerpts modulates.

a. From *Little Prelude No. 1* by J.S. Bach.
   Original key: C Major. Modulates to: _____

b. From *Sonatina, Op. 36, No. 3* by Clementi.
   Original key: C Major. Modulates to: _____

c. From *Little Prelude No. 2* by J.S. Bach.
   Original key: c minor. Modulates to: _____

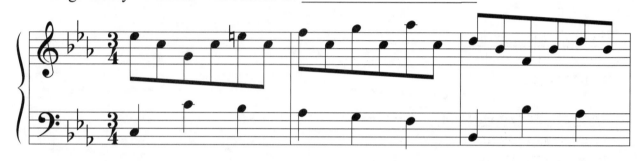

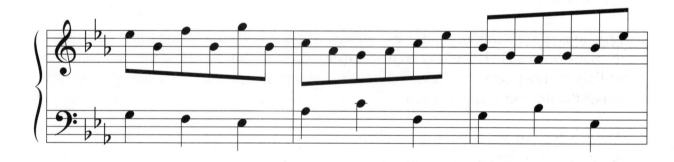

LESSON 13
THE FOUR PERIODS OF MUSIC HISTORY
THE BAROQUE PERIOD

The history of music since 1600 is divided into four periods:

Baroque:	**1600-1750**
Classical:	**1750-1830**
Romantic:	**1830-1900**
Contemporary:	**1900-present**

Music of the **BAROQUE PERIOD** (1600-1750) is characterized by the following:

a. **Polyphonic Texture:** Two or more separate voices are interchanged to create the music. The melodies are passed between the parts, and the parts are of equal importance.

b. **Use of Ornamentation:** Composers included many trills, mordents, and other ornaments in their music. It was the performer's responsibility to know how to play the ornaments correctly. Performers could also add their own ornaments at appropriate places in the music.

c. **Improvisation:** Not only did music of the Baroque Period contain many ornaments, the performer was also free to improvise sections of the music. This not only included adding the ornaments mentioned above, but also playing **Cadenzas**, entire sections of music that the performer created, often after a cadence in the music.

Another type of improvisation in Baroque music was the use of **Figured Bass.** The performer was given an outline of the chord progression of a composition. The performer improvised using the harmonies specified by the figured bass.

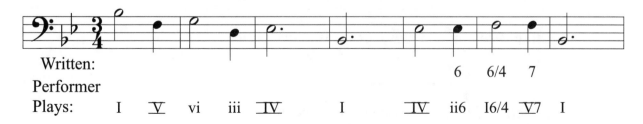

FIGURED BASS

d Most keyboard music of the Baroque Period was written for the **harpsichord, clavichord**, and **organ**. The piano was not invented and perfected until late in the Baroque Period.

e. **Terraced Dynamics:** Since much of the keyboard music from the Baroque Period was written for the harpsichord, which does not have the capability of making crescendos or diminuendos, performers used terraced dynamics. This takes place when the dynamics increase or decrease by sections: *p mp mf f*, rather than gradually. (This type of dynamic contrast is most prevalent in keyboard music of the period. Other instruments, such as the violin, did create true crescendos and decrescendos during the Baroque Period.)

This example, from *Short Prelude No. 7* by J.S. Bach, shows these characteristics: Polyphonic texture and terraced dynamics.

Answer these questions.

1. Most keyboard music of the Baroque period was written for which three instruments?

   _____

2. Describe two types of imporvisation used in Baroque music.

   _____

3. What type of ornamentation was used in Baroque music?

   _____

4. What texture is common in music of the Baroque period?

   _____

5. Why were terraced dynamics used in Baroque music?

   _____

JOHANN SEBASTIAN BACH

Johann Sebastian Bach was born in 1685 in Germany, into a very musical family. He spent most of his adult life (from age 38 to his death at age 65) as musical director and organist at St. Thomas' School in Leipzig, Germany. He was never wealthy, and was not to become famous until about 100 years after his death, when his music, which had been "forgotten," was rediscovered by another German composer, Felix Mendlessohn.

Bach wrote an abundance of music for choir, orchestra, and keyboard. Although we perform much of Bach's music on the piano now, Bach did not actually write music for piano. He wrote it for other keyboard instruments: the harpsichord, clavichord, and organ. His keyboard works include a great deal of polyphonic music, such as two-part *Inventions*, three-part *Sinfonias*, preludes and fugues (the *Short Preludes and Fugues* and *Well-Tempered Clavier, Books 1 and 2* are good examples), *Toccatas*, *French and English Suites*, and *Partitas*. Bach's keyboard music encompasses a variety of levels, from beginning to virtuoso.

J.S. Bach also wrote many other works, including cantatas and passions (choral works), and the *Brandenburg Concertos* (for strings and harpsichord).

Answer these questions.

1. Where was Bach born? _____

2. During which period of music history did Bach live? _____

3. For which keyboard instruments did Bach write? _____

_____

4. What did Bach do for a living most of his life? _____

_____

5. Was Bach famous during his lifetime? _____

6. Name some of Bach's keyboard works. _____

_____

_____

Other Baroque composers include:

Domenico Scarlatti, born in Italy

G.F. Handel, born in Germany

LESSON 14
THE CLASSICAL PERIOD

The **CLASSICAL PERIOD** of music took place from approximately 1750-1830. Music from the Classical Period includes the following characteristics:

a. **Homophonic Texture:** Much of the music of the Classical Period has an obvious melody.

b. **Harmonic structure easily recognizable:** Quite often, the harmony of a piece from the Classical Period is easy to hear, uncluttered by extra notes.

c. **Rests:** Before a new theme or sections is introduced, rests are often used to set off the new section.

d. **Alberti Bass:** A common type of accompaniment for the left hand part of piano music from the Classical Period is Alberti Bass, a repeated pattern in this style:

ALBERTI BASS

e. **Sonata and Sonatina forms:** A sonata or sonatina may contain several movements (usually two, three, or four), with the first movement having an **Exposition, Development**, and **Recapitulation.** When there are three movements, the second is usually a slow movement in a different but related key, and the third is often a Rondo (ABACABA form), in the same key as the first movement.

This example, from *Sonatina, Op. 36, No. 3* by Clementi, shows these characteristics: Homophonic texture, clear melody and harmony, and use of rests.

Answer these questions.

1. What form was developed during the Classical Period? _____

2. What type of texture is common in music of the Classical Period? _____

3. Name the repeated bass pattern developed during the Classical Period. _____

_____

4. What is one way that composers of the Classical Period used rests? _____

_____

5. Describe the way in which melody and harmony are used in music of the Classical

Period. _____

WOLFGANG AMADEUS MOZART

Wolfgang Amadeus Mozart lived during the Classical Period, and is well known

for his life as a child prodigy. He was playing piano and composing at the early age of

four, and traveled throughout Europe with his sister Nanerl (also a good musician) and

his violin teacher father, Leopold. Mozart was born in the town of Salzburg, Austria.

For a few years, Mozart worked for the Archbishop of Salzburg as a court musician, but

he was unable to get along with his unbearable employer. After leaving the job at age 25,

Mozart spent the rest of his short life composing and performing, making his living as a

professional composer. He was the first well known composer to do this, and was one of

the last court musicians.

Despite a rigorous teaching and performing schedule, Mozart was able to compose an abundance of music, ranging from simple minuets to many piano concertos and symphonies. He also wrote choral works, operas, piano sonatas, and works for solo instruments.

Mozart died in his early thirties, and was buried in a common grave. Despite his untimely death, Mozart was able to produce an great deal of wonderful music.

Answer these questions.

1. During which period of music did Mozart live? _____

2. What two jobs did Mozart have during his lifetime? What is unique about one of these jobs? _____

_____

3. What was special about Mozart's childhood? _____

_____

4. Where was Mozart born? _____

FRANZ JOSEF HAYDN

Franz Josef Haydn also lived during the Classical Period of music history, but his lifestyle was much different from Mozart's. He was born in Austria, near the Hungarian border, but studied music (as a choirboy) in Vienna from the early age of 8. Haydn loved practical jokes, and was expelled from the Vienna school after he cut off a fellow student's pigtail while trying out a new pair of scissors. By this time, Haydn was old enough (in his late teens) to make his own living as a composer. He wrote a great deal of music, and was soon hired as full time Director of Music to Prince Esterhazy at Eisenstadt.

Unlike Mozart, Haydn had a good salary, and was able to compose and have his music performed as often as he liked. He was one of the first composers to begin developing Sonata Allegro form.

His love of practical jokes can be heard in his music. His *Farewell Symphony* was written at a time when the court musicians were overdue for a vacation. To remind Prince Esterhazy of this, Haydn arranged the music so that each musician leaves the stage when his part is over. By the end of the symphony, there are two lone musicians left.

In his *Surprise Symphony*, the second movement (the slow movement) has a carefully placed sudden sforzando after a quiet opening, to wake sleepy audiences.

Haydn is best known for being the "Father of the Symphony," or "Papa Haydn," having written over 100 symphonies. He developed the standard four movement format for symphonies. He also wrote much chamber music and many piano sonatas, as well as varied works for other instruments and choir

Answer these questions.

1. Where did Haydn spend his childhood? _____

2. What did Haydn do for a living? _____

3. What two forms did Haydn develop? _____

4. Discuss Haydn's practical jokes in life and music. _____

_____

_____

_____

_____

5. During which period of music history did Haydn live? _____

LUDWIG VAN BEETHOVEN

Ludwig van Beethoven is probably the most famous of all composers. He wrote a great deal of music for piano, orchestra, and solo instruments. Although he usually is considered a Classical composer, he actually was in the transition between the Classical and Romantic periods. He wrote using Classical forms, but gave them new richness. He developed Sonata Allegro form into a deeper, more complicated form, and paved the way for the grandeur of Romantic orchestral works with his nine symphonies.

Beethoven was born in Bonn, Germany, in 1770, but spent most of his life in Vienna, Austria. He made his living as a teacher and composer. Tragedy struck his life when he lost his hearing around age 30. Despite this, he continued composing, and some of his greatest works were written after he went deaf.

Beethoven wrote 32 piano sonatas, five piano concertos, nine symphonies, and an abundance of other music, which includes several string quartets, choral music, and an opera.

Answer these questions.

1. Name one of Beethoven's contributions to musical style. _____

   _____

2. Did Beethoven write music after he went deaf? _____

3. How did Beethoven make his living? _____

4. Which two periods of music does Beethoven represent? _____

LESSON 15
THE ROMANTIC PERIOD

The **ROMANTIC PERIOD** of music took place from approximately 1830-1900. Music of the Romantic Period is the most popular of the four periods of music history. Some characteristics of this music are:

a. **Music became more emotional:** Much of the music of the Romantic period was written about things, people, places, or feelings. The titles in music of the period reflect the mood of the piece (such as *The Merry Farmer* by Schumann, *To a Wild Rose* by MacDowell, or *Elfin Dance* by Grieg).

b. **Harmonies more complicated:** Composers began to add more colorful notes to their chords, using more chromaticism, and straying from the tonal scale.

c. **Lyric melodies:** Many of the melodies in music of the Romantic period are lovely, singing melodies that have become favorites among music lovers.

d. **Rhythms more complicated:** Music of the Romantic period contains many syncopated rhythms, complicated sixteenth note and dotted note combinations, triplets, cross rhythms (two against three), etc.

This example, from *Reaper's Song* by Schumann, shows these characteristics: A descriptive title, more complex chords, more complicated rhythms, lyric melody.

Answer these questions.

1. What types of titles are often used in music of the Romantic period? _____

_____

2. What changes took place in the harmonies of the music during the Romantic period?

_____

3. What type of melodies occur in music from the Romantic period? _____

_____

4. Describe some types of rhythms used in Romantic music. _____

_____

EDVARD GRIEG

Born in Norway, **<u>Edvard Grieg</u>** lived during the Romantic period. He wrote a good deal of music which represents his nation, using folk tunes of his country. His *Piano Concerto* and *Peer Gynt Suite* are probably his most famous works, but he also wrote other music for orchestra and solo instruments.

Grieg did not live in Norway all his life, but studied music in Germany. Despite his German training, his music still has a Norwegian flavor.

Answer these questions.

1. During which period of music history did Grieg live? _____

2. Where was Grieg born, and how did this affect his music? _____

_____

_____

3. Where did Grieg study music? _____

4. Name two of Grieg's famous compositions. _____

_____

ROBERT SCHUMANN

Robert Schumann is one of the best known Romantic composers. Born in Germany in 1810, he wrote a great deal of piano music, which varies in difficulty from the *Album for the Young* for beginning students, to several very difficult virtuoso pieces. Schumann studied to be a lawyer, according to his family's wishes, but his desire to write and perform music eventually drew his away from law. He married Clara Wieck, the daughter of his piano teacher, who was also an excellent pianist. Legend has it that Schumann permanently crippled his hand in an attempt to strengthen his fourth finger with a pulley device, but some historians now believe that he had tendonitis (a problem caused by overuse of the hands). After this, Clara often performed his piano works for audiences.

Schumann edited a musical journal called the *Neue Zeitschrift für Musik (New Journal of Music)*, one of the first of its kind. He wrote a variety of music, including symphonies, a piano concerto, an opera, chamber music, songs, and violin concertos, but most of his works are for piano.

In his later years, Schumann became mentally ill due to a hereditary disease, and spent several years of his life in a mental institution, a tragic end to a creative and productive life.

Answer these questions.

1. Who performed Schumann's music for him after his hand became crippled?

_____

2. For which instrument did Schumann write much of his music? _____

3. Name the collection of music by Schumann for beginning piano students. _____

   _____

4. What was the *Neue Zeitschrift für Musik*, and what did Schumann have to do with it?

   _____

   _____

5. What nationality was Schumann? _____

6. During which period of music did Schumann live? _____

LESSON 16
THE CONTEMPORARY PERIOD

Many changes have taken place in the way music sounds during the **Contemporary Period (1900-present).**

a. **Major and minor tonalities avoided**, with non-tonal (not in Major or minor keys) harmonies being used.

b. **Quartal Harmony:** The use of 4ths to make up chords, rather than thirds.

QUARTAL HARMONY

c. **Bitonality:** The use of two different keys at the same time.

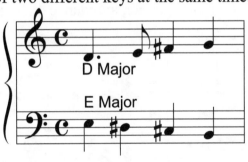

BITONALITY

d. **Polytonality:** The use of many different keys at the same time.

POLYTONALITY

e. **Atonality:** No specific key used.

ATONALITY

f. **Irregular and changing meters:** Composers often use uncommon time signatures such as 5/4 or 7/4, or change the time signature during the course of the music (complex meter).

g. **Polyphonic texture:** This texture is often used, with the harmonies becoming the result of the entangling of the melodic lines.

h. **Use of Classical forms:** Composers often write Sonatas, Sonatinas, or other forms which were common during the Classical Period.

This example, from *Evening in the Country* by Bartok, shows these characteristics: polyphonic texture, changing (complex) meter, avoidance of Major and minor tonalities.

Answer these questions.

1. Give the name for each of these types of tonality:

a. _____ Two separate keys played at the same time.

b. _____ 4ths used for harmonies (rather than 3rds).

c. _____ No specific key used.

d. _____ Several different keys played at the same time.

2. What has happened to Major and minor tonalities in music of the Contemporary Period? _____

_____

3. What types of meters are used in music of the Contemporary Period? _____

_____

4. What is a common texture used in music of the Contemporary Period? _____

_____

5. What forms are often used in this music? _____

_____

DMITRI KABALEVSKY

Dmitri Kabalevsky was born in 1904, in St. Petersburg, Russia. He was a Contemporary composer. His father wanted him to become a mathematician, and until he was 18, Kabalevsky worked toward that goal. He did not even begin piano lessons until he was 14 years old. When he was 18, he decided to become a professional pianist. He studied music at the Moscow Conservatory.

Kabalevsky wrote numerous pieces for children. Many of these were written for his own piano students. He also wrote many orchestral and vocal works. His Second Piano Concerto is one of his most famous works. He also wrote incidental music for stage plays and radio.

The music of Kabalevsky is influenced by the folk music of his homeland, Russia. Many of his songs were patriotic, written during times of war.

Kabalevsky taught at the Moscow Conservatory, and was famous as a composer, teacher, administrator, and writer.

Answer these questions.

1. Where was Kabalevsky born? _____

2. At what age did Kabalevsky get a start on his musical career? _____

3. What elements of Russia influenced Kabalevsky's music? _____

   _____

4. For what was Kabalevsky famous besides composing music? _____

   _____

BELA BARTOK

Bela Bartok was a Contemporary composer. He was Hungarian, and his music shows the influences of Hungarian folk music. Bartok was innovative in his composing, being one of the first composers to write using untraditional sounds. His *Mikrokosmos* are a set of beginning piano pieces which demonstrate this new style.

Bartok wrote a variety of music, including beginning and advanced piano music, piano concertos, string quartets, and several orchestral works.

Answer these questions.

1. How does Bartok's music differ from that of the composers before him? _____

   _____

2. What nationality was Bartok, and how did that affect his music? _____

   _____

3. What are Bartok's *Mikrokosmos*? _____

4. During which musical period did Bartok live? _____

REVIEW
LESSONS 8-16

1. Write the counts for each example below, and place accents on the strong beats.

a. From *Mazurka* by Tchaikovsky

b. From *Album Leaf* by Grieg.

c. From *Tarantella* by Prokofiev.

2. Define these terms.

a. *fp* _____

b. doloroso _____

c. Opus _____

d. Syncopation _____

e. robusto _____

f. scherzando _____

g. sostenuto _____

h. marcato _____

i. simile _____

j. 𝄪 _____

k. ♭♭ _____

3. Circle the repetition, imitation, or sequence in each of these examples, and write the type of technique on the line above the music.

a. From *Minuet in G* by Beethoven. _____

b. From *Sonatina, Op. 55, No. 1*, by Kuhlau. _____

c. From *Little Prelude No. 9* by J.S. Bach. _____

4. What term is used for a key change within a composition? _____

5. Transpose this melody to the key of E Major. Write the transposition on the blank staff.

6. Name the four periods of music history and their approximate dates.

_____   _____

_____   _____

_____   _____

_____   _____

7. Mark these statements with T for true, and F for false.

a. _____ Beethoven represents the Classical period.

b. _____ Kabalevsky was Norwegian.

c. _____ J.S. Bach was a Baroque composer.

d. _____ Edvard Grieg represents the Romantic period.

e. _____ Classical forms are used in music of the Contemporary period.

f. _____ Music of the Baroque period should never be played with added ornaments.

g. _____ Alberti Bass was developed during the Classical period.

h. _____ Contemporary music consists mainly of Major and minor tonalities.

i. _____ During the Classical period, music was very colorful, with descriptive titles.

Score: _____   **REVIEW TEST**   Perfect Score = 87
Passing Score = 60

1. Write the names of the Major and minor keys for each of these key signatures. (8 points)

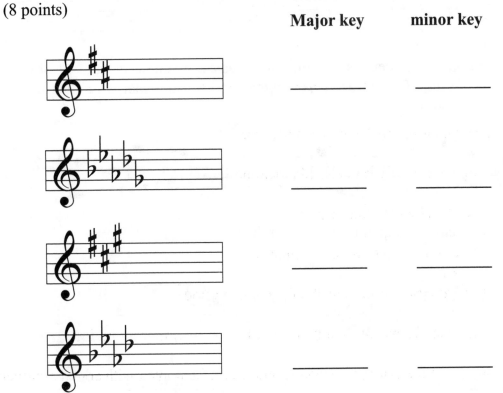

	Major key	minor key
	_____	_____
	_____	_____
	_____	_____
	_____	_____

2. Write the key signature for each of the following keys. (4 points)

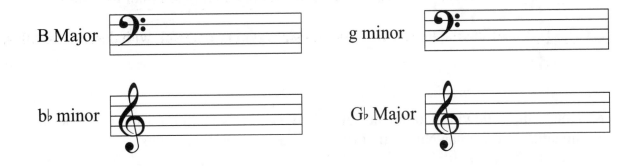

B Major

g minor

b♭ minor

G♭ Major

3. Add the correct accidentals needed to make the A♭ Major scale. (Do not use a key signature. Put the necessary sharps or flats before the notes.) (1 point)

4. a. Add the correct accidentals to make the f minor scale, natural form. (Do not use a key signature. Put the sharps or flats before the notes.) (1 point)

   b. Add the correct accidentals to make this musical example in the key of c minor, harmonic form. (Do not use a key signature. Put the sharps or flats before the notes.) (1 point)

5. Give the letter name and quality for each of these triads. (The first one is given.) (5 points)

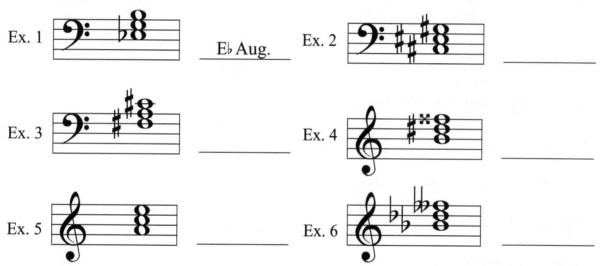

Ex. 1   E♭ Aug.   Ex. 2 _____

Ex. 3 _____   Ex. 4 _____

Ex. 5 _____   Ex. 6 _____

6. Notate the following Dominant Seventh (V7) chords in root position. Write the key signature and Roman Numeral. (The first one is given.) (5 points)

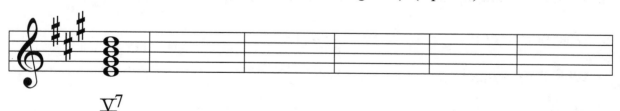

V⁷

Key of: A Major   e minor   D Major   g minor   E♭ Major   c minor

7. The following example is from a Sonata by Scarlatti. Answer the questions about the music. (10 points)

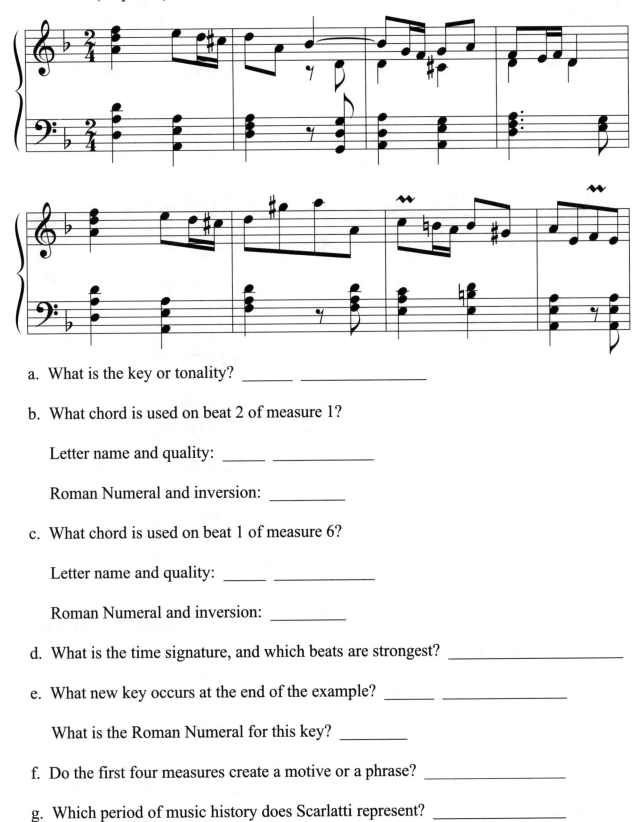

a. What is the key or tonality? _____ _____

b. What chord is used on beat 2 of measure 1?

Letter name and quality: _____ _____

Roman Numeral and inversion: _____

c. What chord is used on beat 1 of measure 6?

Letter name and quality: _____ _____

Roman Numeral and inversion: _____

d. What is the time signature, and which beats are strongest? _____

e. What new key occurs at the end of the example? _____ _____

What is the Roman Numeral for this key? _____

f. Do the first four measures create a motive or a phrase? _____

g. Which period of music history does Scarlatti represent? _____

8. Define the following musical terms. (8 points)

a. doloroso   _____   e. con brio   _____

b. sostenuto   _____   f. simile   _____

c. marcato   _____   g. scherzando _____

d. robusto   _____   h. leggiero   _____

9. The example below is from *Dance, Op. 60, No. 2,* by Kabalevsky. Answer the questions about the music. (11 points)

a. What is the key or tonality? _____ _____

b. What compositional technique occurs using the first motive? _____

c. What is the time signature? _____

d. Name the circled intervals. Give the quality and number.

1. _____ 2. _____ 3. _____ 4. _____ 5. _____ 6. _____

e. What type of scale movement is used in measure 5-8? _____

f. What period of music does Kabalevsky represent? _____

10. Write the Roman Numerals (including inversions) for the following chord progression. (4 points)

_____   _____   _____   _____   _____

11. The following example is from a Bagatelle by Beethoven. Answer the questions about the music. (13 points)

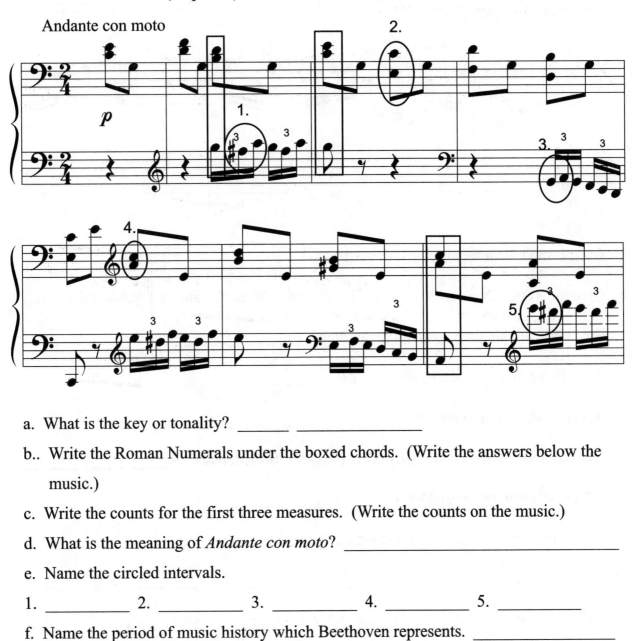

a. What is the key or tonality? _____ _____

b.. Write the Roman Numerals under the boxed chords. (Write the answers below the music.)

c. Write the counts for the first three measures. (Write the counts on the music.)

d. What is the meaning of *Andante con moto*? _____

e. Name the circled intervals.

1. _____   2. _____   3. _____   4. _____   5. _____

f. Name the period of music history which Beethoven represents. _____

12. The following example is from *Solfegietto* by C.P.E. Bach. Answer the questions about the music. (8 points)

Allegro Vivace

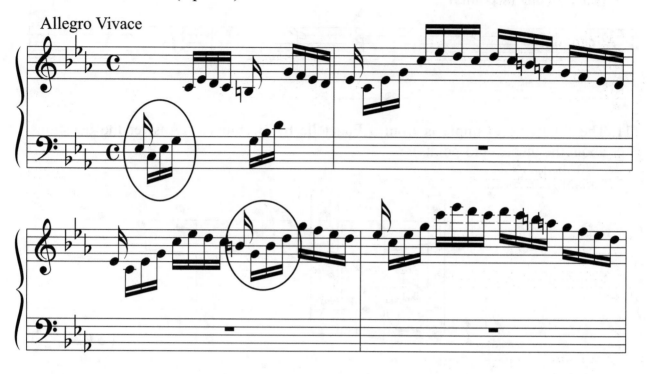

a. What is the key or tonality? _____ _____

b. Give the Roman Numerals of the circled chords. (Write the answers below the music.)

c. How else can this time signature be written? _____

d. What is the meaning of *Allegro Vivace*? _____

e. Which beats are strongest? _____

f. C.P.E. Bach is from the same period as Mozart. Name this period and one other

   composer from the same period.

   _____   _____

13. The following example is from *Puck* by Grieg. Answer the questions about the music. (8 points)

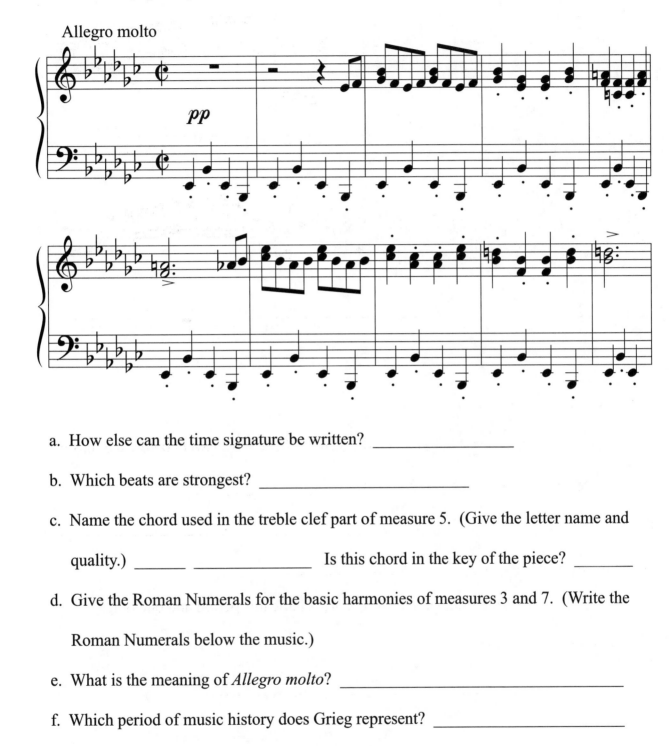

a. How else can the time signature be written? _____

b. Which beats are strongest? _____

c. Name the chord used in the treble clef part of measure 5. (Give the letter name and

   quality.) _____ _____ Is this chord in the key of the piece? _____

d. Give the Roman Numerals for the basic harmonies of measures 3 and 7. (Write the

   Roman Numerals below the music.)

e. What is the meaning of *Allegro molto*? _____

f. Which period of music history does Grieg represent? _____

REFERENCES

Apel, Willi. *Harvard Dictionary of Music, Second Edition.* Cambridge, Massachusetts: Belknap Press of Harvard University Press, 1972.

Arnold, Denis, ed. *The New Oxford Companion to Music, Volumes 1 and 2.* New York: Oxford University Press, 1983.

Music Teachers' Association of California. *Certificate of Merit Piano Syllabus, 1992 Edition.* San Francisco: Music Teachers' Association of California, 1992.

Music Teachers' Association of California. *Certificate of Merit Piano Syllabus, 1997 Edition.* Ontario, Canada: The Frederick Harris Music Company, Limited, 1997.

Sadie, Stanley, ed. *The New Grove Dictionary of Music and Musicians.* Washington, D.C.: Grove's Dictionaries of Music Inc., 1980.

BASICS OF KEYBOARD THEORY

Workbooks by Julie McIntosh Johnson
Computer Activities by Nancy Plourde

NAME _____

ADDRESS _____

CITY_____ STATE_____ ZIP_____

PHONE _____ E-MAIL_____

QTY	ITEM	COST	TOTAL
	PREPARATORY LEVEL	**9.50**	
	LEVEL 1	**9.50**	
	LEVEL 2	**9.50**	
	LEVEL 3	**9.95**	
	LEVEL 4	**9.95**	
	LEVEL 5	**10.50**	
	LEVEL 6	**10.50**	
	LEVEL 7	**10.95**	
	LEVEL 8	**11.95**	
	LEVEL 9	**12.95**	
	Level 10 (Advanced)	**12.50**	
	ANSWER BOOK	**11.95**	
	COMPUTER ACTIVITIES LEVELS PREP-2, Mac/PC	**49.95**	
	COMPUTER ACTIVITIES LEVELS 3-4, Mac/PC	**39.95**	
	COMPUTER ACTIVITIES LEVELS 5-6, PC Only	**49.95**	

Shipping:
   1-5 Books.........$5.00
   6-10 Books.......$6.00
   11 or more........$7.00

Sub-Total	
Calif. Residents: Sales Tax	
Shipping	
TOTAL	

Make checks payable to:

J. Johnson Music Publications

5062 Siesta Lane

Yorba Linda, CA 92886

714-961-0257   www.bktmusic.com   info@bktmusic.com